THE BOOK OF GOOD COUNSELS

FROM THE SANSKRIT OF

HITOPADESA

THE BOOK OF GOOD COUNSELS

FROM THE SANSKRIT OF

HITOPADESA

SIR EDWIN ARNOLD

Author of

THE LIGHT OF ASIA
THE LIGHT OF THE WORLD

Illustrations by
CORDON BROWNE

GYAN

Published by

Gyan Publishing House
5, Ansari Road
Daryaganj, New Delhi-110002
Phone: 011-47034999, 9811692060
E-mail: books@gyanbooks.com

Distribution Network
gyanbooks.com
India, USA, Canada, UK, Australia, France

ISBN : 978-81-212-3153-4 (PB)
First Published, 1924

2nd Impression 2020

Printed at: Gyan Press, Delhi.

The Book of Good Counsels
Author: Edwin Arnold

Dedication

TO FIRST EDITION.

To you, dear Wife—to whom beside so well?—
  True Counsellor and tried, at every shift,
I bring my "Book of Counsels:" let it tell
  Largeness of love by littleness of gift:

And take this growth of foreign skies from me,
  (A scholar's thanks for gentle help in toil,)
Whose leaf, "though dark," like Milton's Hoemony,
  "Bears a bright golden flower, if not in this soil."

PREFACE TO NEW EDITION.

I MADE this book of Indian stories and poetical maxims, from the Sanskrit, more than thirty years ago, in India. The work has passed out of print; yet, as it seems a pity that the pretty forest fables and curious quotations from Indian poetry which it contains should be lost, I republish the pages, with very few alterations, but in another and a more popular form.

EDWIN ARNOLD.

LONDON,
September, 1893.

PREFACE.

A STORY-BOOK from the Sanskrit at least possesses the minor merit of novelty. The "perfect language" has been hitherto regarded as the province of Scholars, and few of these even have found time or taste to search its treasures. And yet among them is the key to the heart of modern India—as well as the splendid record of her ancient Gods and glories. The hope of Hindostan lies in the intelligent interest of England. Whatever avails to dissipate misconceptions between them, and to enlarge their intimacy, is a gain to both Peoples; and to this end the present volume aspires, in an humble degree, to contribute.

The "Hitopadesa" is a work of high antiquity, and extended popularity. The prose is doubtless as old as our own era; but the intercalated verses and proverbs compose a selection from writings of an age extremely remote. The "Mahabharata" and the textual "Veds" are of those quoted: to the first of which Professor M. Williams (in his admirable edition of the "Nala," 1860) assigns a date of 350 B.C., while he claims for the "Rig-Veda" an antiquity as high as 1300 B.C. The "Hitopadesa" may thus be fairly styled "The Father of all Fables;" for from its numerous translations have come

Esop and Pilpay, and in latter days "Reineke Fuchs." Originally compiled in Sanskrit, it was rendered, by order of Nushiraván, in the sixth century A.D. into Persic. From the Persic it passed, A.D. 850, into the Arabic, and thence into Hebrew and Greek. In its own land it obtained as wide a circulation. The Emperor Akbar, impressed with the wisdom of its maxims and the ingenuity of its apologues, commended the work of translating it to his own Vizier, Abdul Fazel. That Minister accordingly put the book into a familiar style, and published it with explanations, under the title of the "Criterion of Wisdom." The Emperor had also suggested the abridgment of the long series of shlokes which here and there interrupt the narrative, and the Vizier found such advice sound, and followed it, like the present Translator. To this day, in India, the "Hitopadesa," under other names (as the "Anvári Suhaili [1]), retains the delighted attention of young and old, and has some representative in all the Indian vernaculars. A work so well esteemed in the East cannot be unwelcome to Western readers, who receive it here, in a condensed but faithful transcript of sense and manner.

As often as an Oriental allusion, or a name in Hindoo mythology, seemed to ask some explanation for the English reader, notes have been appended, bearing reference to the page. In their compilation, and generally, acknowledgment is due to Professor Johnson's excellent version and edition of the "Hitopadesa," and to Mr. Muir's "Sanskrit Texts."

A residence in India, and close intercourse with the

[1] "The lights of Canopus," a Persian paraphrase; as the *Khirad Afroz*, "the lamp of the Understanding," is in Hindustani.

Hindoos, has given the Author a lively desire to subserve their advancement. No one listens now to the precipitate ignorance which would set aside as "heathenish" the high civilization of this great race; but justice is not yet done to their past development and present capacities. If the wit, the morality, and the philosophy of these "animals of India," surprise any vigorous mind into further exploration of her literature, and deeper sense of our responsibility in her government, the Author will be repaid.

E. A.

CONTENTS.

PAGE

PREFACE TO NEW EDITION vii

PREFACE ix

INTRODUCTION 17

THE WINNING OF FRIENDS.

1. The Story of the Tiger and the Traveller . . . 23
2. The Story of the Jackal, Deer, and Crow . . . 30
3. The Story of the Vulture, the Cat, and the Birds . . 32
4. The Story of the Dead Game and the Jackal . . . 45
5. The Prince and the Wife of the Merchant's Son . . 49
6. The Story of the Old Jackal and the Elephant . . 50

THE PARTING OF FRIENDS.

1. The Story of the Lion, the Jackals, and the Bull . . 55
2. The Story of the Monkey and the Wedge . . . 59
3. The Story of the Washerman's Jackass 60
4. The Story of the Cat who served the Lion . . . 67
5. The Story of the Terrible Bell 69
6. The Story of the Prince and the Procuress who suffered for their own Faults 73
7. The Story of the Black Snake and the Golden Chain . 76
8. The Story of the Lion and the Old Hare 77
9. The Story of the Wagtail and the Sea 82

WAR.

1. The Battle of the Swans and Peacocks 87
2. The Story of the Weaver Birds and the Monkeys . . 89
3. The Story of the Old Hare and the Elephants . . 91
4. The Story of the Heron and the Crow 94

PAGE

5. The Story of the Appeased Wheelwright 95
6. The Story of the Dyed Jackal 100
7. The Story of the Faithful Rajpoot 104

PEACE.

1. The Treaty between the Peacocks and the Swans . . 115
2. The Story of the Tortoise and the Geese 116
3. The Story of Fate and the Three Fishes 118
4. The Story of the Unabashed Wife 118
5. The Story of the Herons and the Mongoose 120
6. The Story of the Recluse and the Mouse 122
7. The Story of the Crane and the Crab 123
8. The Story of the Brahman and the Pans 125
9. The Duel of the Giants 127
10. The Story of the Brahman and the Goat 131
11. The Story of the Camel, the Lion, and his Court . . 132
12. The Story of the Frogs and the Old Serpent . . . 135

NOTES 143

LIST OF ILLUSTRATIONS.

PAGE

The Lion, the Jackals, and the Bull . . . *Frontispiece*
The Winning of Friends (Initial) 21
The Tiger and the Traveller 25
The Jackal, Deer, and Crow 31
The Vulture, the Cat, and the Birds 33
" " " . . . . . *To face* 35
" " " 40
The Dead Game and the Jackal . . . . . *To face* 45
The Old Jackal and the Elephant 51
" " " 52
The Lion, the Jackals, and the Bull 57
The Monkey and the Wedge . . . . . *To face* 59
The Terrible Bell 70
The Prince and the Procuress who suffered for their own faults . . . . *To face* 74
The Lion and the Old Hare 78
The Faithful Rajpoot . . . . . . *To face* 105
The Tortoise and the Geese 117
The Herons and the Mongoose . . . . *To face* 121
The Crane and the Crab 124
The Frogs and the Old Serpent 135

THE

BOOK OF GOOD COUNSELS.

INTRODUCTION.

Honour to Gunesh,(1) God of Wisdom.

This book of Counsel read, and you shall see
Fair speech and Sanskrit lore, and Policy.

ON the banks of the holy river Ganges there stood a city named Pataliputra (2). The King of it was a good King and a virtuous, and his name was Sudarsana. It chanced one day that he overheard a certain person reciting these verses—

"Wise men, holding wisdom highest, scorn delights, more false than fair,
Daily live they as Death's fingers twined already in their hair.

Truly, richer than all riches, better than the best of gain,
Wisdom is. Unbought, secure—once won, none loseth her again.

Bringing dark things into daylight, solving doubts that vex the mind,
Like an open eye is wisdom—he that hath her not is blind."

Hearing these the King became disquieted, knowing that his own sons were gaining no wisdom, nor reading the

Sacred Writings (3), but altogether going in the wrong way; and he repeated this verse to himself—

"Childless art thou (4)? dead thy children? leaving thee to want and dool?
Less thy misery than his is, who is father to a fool."

And again this,—

"One wise son makes glad his father, forty fools avail him not:
One moon silvers all that darkness which the silly stars did dot."

"And it has been said," reflected he,—

"Ease and health, obeisant children, wisdom, and a fair-voiced wife—
Thus, great King! are counted up the five felicities of life.

For the son the sire is honoured; though the bow-cane bendeth true,
Let the strained string crack in using, and what service shall it do?"

"Nevertheless," mused the King, "I know it is urged that human efforts are useless: as, for instance,—

"That which will not be, will not be—and what is to be, will be:
Why not drink this easy physic, antidote of misery?"

"But then that comes from idleness, with people who will not do what they should do. Rather say:—

"Nay! and faint not, idly sighing, 'Destiny is mightiest,'
Sesamum (5) holds oil in plenty, but it yieldeth none unpressed.

Ah! it is the Coward's babble, 'Fortune taketh, Fortune gave;'
Fortune! rate her like a master, and she serves thee like a slave."

"For indeed,

"Two-fold is the life we live in—Fate and Will together run:
Two wheels bear life's chariot onward—will it move on only one?"

"And again:—

"Look! the clay dries into iron, but the potter moulds the clay:
Destiny to-day is master—Man was master yesterday."

"So verily,

"Worthy ends come not by wishing. Wouldst thou? Up, and win it, then!
While the hungry lion slumbers, not a deer comes to his den."

Having concluded his reflections, the Raja gave orders to assemble a meeting of learned men. Then said he in their midst,—

"Hear now, O my Pundits (6)! Is there one among you so wise that he will undertake to give the second birth of Wisdom to these my sons, by teaching them the Books of Policy; for they have never yet read the Sacred Writings, and are altogether going in the wrong road; and ye know that

"Silly glass, in splendid settings, something of the gold may gain;
And in company of wise ones, fools to wisdom may attain."

Then uprose a great Sage, by name Vishnu-Sarman, learned in the principles of Policy as is the angel of the planet Jupiter (7) himself, and he said,—

"My Lord King, I will undertake to teach these princes Policy, seeing they are born of a great house; for—

"Labours, spent on the unworthy, of reward the labourer balk;
Like the parrot, teach the heron twenty times, he will not talk."

"But in this royal family the offspring are royal-minded, and in six moons I will engage to make your Majesty's sons comprehend Policy."

The Raja replied, with condescension:—

"On the eastern mountains lying, common things shine in the sun,
And, by learned minds enlightened, lower minds may show as one."

"And you, worshipful sir, are competent to teach my children the rules of Policy."

So saying, with much graciousness, he gave the Princes into the charge of Vishnu-Sarman; and that sage, by way of introduction, spake to the Princes, as they sat at ease on the balcony of the palace, in this wise:—

"Hear now, my Princes! for the delectation of your Highnesses, I purpose to tell the tale of the Crow, the Tortoise, the Deer, and the Mouse."

"Pray, sir," said the King's sons, "let us hear it."

Vishnu-Sarman answered,—

"It begins with the Winning of Friends; and this is the first verse of it:—

> "*Sans* way or wealth, wise friends their purpose gain—
> The Mouse, Crow, Deer, and Tortoise make this plain."

The Winning of Friends.

“Sans *way or wealth, wise friends their purpose gain—*
The Mouse, Crow, Deer, and Tortoise make this plain.”

HOWEVER was that?” asked the Princes.

Vishnu-Sarman replied:—

“On the banks of the Godavery there stood a large silk-cotton-tree ([8]), and thither at night, from all quarters and regions, the birds came to roost. Now once, when the night was just spent, and his Radiance the Moon ([9]), Lover of the white lotus, was about to retire behind the western hills, a Crow ([10]) who perched there, ‘Light o’ Leap’ by name, upon awakening, saw to his great wonder a fowler approaching—a second God of Death ([11]). The sight set him reflecting, as he flew off uneasily to follow up the man’s movements, and he began to think what mischief this ill-omened apparition foretold.

"For, a thousand thoughts of sorrow, and a hundred things of dread,
By the wise unheeded, trouble day by day the foolish head."

And yet in this life it is true that

"Of the day's impending dangers, Sickness, Death, and Misery,
One will be; the wise man waking, ponders which that one will be."

Presently the fowler fixed a net, scattered grains of rice about, and withdrew to hide. At this moment 'Speckle-neck,' King of the Pigeons, chanced to be passing through the sky with his Court, and caught sight of the rice-grains. Thereupon the King of the Pigeons asked of his rice-loving followers, 'How can there possibly be rice-grains lying here in an unfrequented forest? We will see into it, of course, but We like not the look of it;—love of rice may ruin us, as the Traveller was ruined.

"All out of longing for a golden bangle ([12]),
The Tiger, in the mud, the man did mangle."

"How did that happen?" asked the Pigeons.

The Story of the Tiger and the Traveller.

'THUS,' replied Speckle-neck: 'I was pecking about one day in the Deccan forest, and saw an old tiger (13) sitting newly bathed on the bank of a pool, like a Brahman, and with holy kuskus-grass (14) in his paws.

"Ho! ho! ye travellers," he kept calling out, "take this golden bangle!"

Presently a covetous fellow passed by and heard him.

"Ah!" thought he, "this is a bit of luck—but I must not risk my neck for it either.

"Good things come not out of bad things; wisely leave a longed-for ill;
Nectar being mixed with poison serves no purpose but to kill."

"But all gain is got by risk, so I will see into it at least;" then he called out, "Where is thy bangle?"

The Tiger stretched forth his paw and exhibited it.

"Hem!" said the Traveller, "can I trust such a fierce brute as thou art?"

"Listen," replied the Tiger, "once, in the days of my cubhood, I know I was very wicked. I killed cows, Brahmans, and men (15) without number—and I lost my wife and children for it—and haven't kith or kin left. But lately I met a virtuous man who counselled me to practise the duty of almsgiving—and, as thou seest, I am strict at ablutions and alms. Besides, I am old, and my nails and fangs are gone—so who would mistrust me?

and I have so far conquered selfishness, that I keep this golden bangle for whoso comes. Thou seemest poor! I will give it thee. Is it not said,

"Give to poor men, son of Kûnti ([16])—on the wealthy waste not wealth:
Good are simples for the sick man, good for nought to him in health."

'Wade over the pool, therefore, and take the bangle."

Thereupon the covetous Traveller determined to trust him, and waded into the pool, where he soon found himself plunged in mud, and unable to move.

"Ho! ho!" says the Tiger, "art thou stuck in a slough? stay, I will fetch thee out!"

So saying he approached the wretched man and seized him—who meanwhile bitterly reflected—

"Be his Scripture-learning wondrous, yet the cheat will be a cheat;
Be her pasture ne'er so bitter, yet the cow's milk will be sweet."

And on that verse, too—

"Trust not water, trust not weapons; trust not clawed nor hornëd things;
Neither give thy soul to women, nor thy life to Sons of Kings ([17])."

And those others—

'Look! the Moon, the silver roamer, from whose splendour darkness flies
With his starry cohorts marching, like a crowned king through the skies;
All the grandeur, all the glory, vanish in the Dragon's jaw ([18]);
What is written on the forehead, that will be, and nothing more."

Here his meditations were cut short by the Tiger devouring him. 'And that,' said Speckle-neck, 'is why we counselled caution.'

THE TIGER AND THE TRAVELLER.

'Why, yes!' said a certain pigeon, with some presumption, 'but you've read the verse—

> "Counsel in danger; of it
>   Unwarned, be nothing begun;
> But nobody asks a Prophet
>   Shall the risk of a dinner be run?"

Hearing that, the Pigeons settled at once; for we know that

> "Avarice begetteth anger; blind desires from her begin;
> A right fruitful mother is she of a countless spawn of sin."

And again,

> "Can a golden Deer have being (19)? yet for such the Hero pined:
> When the cloud of danger hovers, then its shadow dims the mind."

Presently they were caught in the net. Thereat, indeed, they all began to abuse the pigeon by whose suggestion they had been ensnared. It is the old tale!

> "Be second and not first!—the share's the same
> If all go well. If not, the Head's to blame."

And we should remember that

> "Passion will be Slave or Mistress: follow her, she brings to woe;
> Lead her, 'tis the way to Fortune. Choose the path that thou wilt go."

When King Speckle-neck heard their reproaches, he said, 'No, no! it is no fault of his;

> "When the time of trouble cometh, friends may oftimes irk us most:
> For the calf at milking-hour the mother's leg is tying-post."

'And in disaster, dismay is a coward's quality; let us rather rely on fortitude, and devise some remedy. How saith the sage?

"In good fortune not elated, in ill-fortune not dismayed,
Ever eloquent in council, never in the fight affrayed—
Proudly emulous of honour, stedfastly on wisdom set;
Perfect virtues in the nature of a noble soul are met.
Whoso hath them, gem and glory of the three wide worlds (20) is he;
Happy mother she that bore him, she who nursed him on her knee."

'Let us do this now directly,' continued the King: 'at one moment and with one will, rising under the net, let us fly off with it: for indeed

"Small things wax exceeding mighty, being cunningly combined:
Furious elephants are fastened with a rope of grass-blades twined."

'And it is written, you know,

"Let the household hold together, though the house be ne'er so small;
Strip the rice-husk from the rice-grain, and it groweth not at all."

Having pondered this advice, the Pigeons adopted it; and flew away with the net. At first the fowler, who was at a distance, hoped to recover them; but as they passed out of sight with the snare about them he gave up the pursuit. Perceiving this, the Pigeons said,

'What is the next thing to be done, O King?'

'A friend of mine,' said Speckle-neck, 'lives near, in a beautiful forest on the Gundaki. Golden-skin is his name—the King of the Mice (21)—he is the one to cut these bonds."

Resolving to have recourse to him, they directed their flight to the hole of Golden-skin—a prudent monarch, who dreaded danger so much that he had made himself a palace with a hundred outlets, and lived always in it. Sitting there he heard the descent of the pigeons, and remained silent and alarmed.

'Friend Golden-skin,' cried the King, 'have you no welcome for us?'

'Ah, my friend!' said the Mouse-king, rushing out on recognizing the voice, 'is it thou art come, Speckle-neck! how delightful!—But what is this?' exclaimed he, regarding the entangled net.

'That,' said King Speckle-neck, 'is the effect of some wrong-doing in a former life,—

"Sickness, anguish, bonds, and woe
Spring from wrongs wrought long ago [22]."

Golden-skin, without replying, ran at once to the net, and began to gnaw the strings that held Speckle-neck.

'Nay! friend, not so,' said the King, 'cut me first these meshes from my followers, and afterwards thou shalt sever mine.'

'I am little,' answered Golden-skin, 'and my teeth are weak—how can I gnaw so much? No! no! I will nibble your strings as long as my teeth last, and afterwards do my best for the others. To preserve dependants by sacrificing oneself is nowhere enjoined by wise moralists; on the contrary,—

"Keep wealth for want, but spend it for thy wife,
And wife, and wealth, and all to guard thy life."

'Friend,' replied King Speckle-neck, 'that may be the rule of policy, but I am one that can by no means bear to witness the distress of those who depend on me, for,—

"Death, that must come, comes nobly when we give
Our wealth, and life, and all, to make men live."

And you know the verse,

"Friend, art thou faithful? guard mine honour so!
And let the earthy rotting body go."

When King Golden-skin heard this answer his heart was charmed, and his fur bristled up for pure pleasure. 'Nobly spoken, friend,' said he, 'nobly spoken! with such a tenderness for those that look to thee, the Sovereignty of the Three Worlds might be fitly thine.' So saying he set himself to cut all their bonds. This done, and the pigeons extricated, the King of the Mice gave them his formal welcome. 'But, your Majesty,' he said, 'this capture in the net was a work of destiny; you must not blame yourself as you did, and suspect a former fault. Is it not written,—

"Floating on his fearless pinions, lost amid the noonday skies,
Even thence the Eagle's vision kens the carcase where it lies;
But the hour that comes to all things comes unto the Lord of Air,
And he rushes, madly blinded, to his ruin in the snare."

With this correction Golden-skin proceeded to perform the duties of hospitality, and afterwards, embracing and dismissing them, the pigeons left for such destination as they fancied, and the King of the Mice retired again into his hole.

Now Light o' Leap, the Crow, had been a spectator of the whole transaction, and wondered at it so much that at last he called out, 'Ho! Golden-skin, thou very laudable Prince, let me too be a friend of thine, and give me thy friendship.'

'Who art thou?' said Golden-skin, who heard him, but would not come out of his hole.

'I am the Crow Light o' Leap,' replied the other.

'How can I possibly be on good terms with thee?' answered Golden-skin with a laugh; 'have you never read,—

"When Food is friends with Feeder, look for Woe,
The Jackal ate the Deer, but for the Crow."

'No! how was that?'

'I will tell thee,' replied Golden-skin:—

The Story of the Jackal, Deer, and Crow.

'FAR away in Behar there is a forest called Champak-Grove (23), and in it had long lived in much affection a Deer and a Crow. The Deer, roaming unrestrained, happy and fat of carcase, was one day descried by a Jackal. "Ho! ho!" thought the Jackal on observing him, "if I could but get this soft meat for a meal! It might be—if I can only win his confidence." Thus reflecting he approached, and saluted him.

"Health be to thee, friend Deer!"

"Who art thou?" said the Deer.

"I'm Small-wit, the Jackal," replied the other. "I live in the wood here, as the dead do, without a friend; but now that I have met with such a friend as thou, I feel as if I were beginning life again with plenty of relations. Consider me your faithful servant."

"Very well," said the Deer; and then, as the glorious King of Day, whose diadem is the light, had withdrawn himself, the two went together to the residence of the Deer. In that same spot, on a branch of champak, dwelt the Crow Sharp-sense, an old friend of the Deer. Seeing them approach together, the Crow said,

"Who is this number two, friend Deer?"

"It is a Jackal," answered the Deer, "that desires our acquaintance."

"You should not become friendly to a stranger without reason," said Sharp-sense. "Don't you know?

"To folks by no one known house-room deny:
The Vulture housed the Cat, and thence did die."

"No! how was that?" said both.

"In this wise," answered the Crow.

The Story of the Vulture, the Cat, and the Birds.

'ON the banks of the Ganges there is a cliff called Vulture-Crag, and thereupon grew a great fig-tree ([24]). It was hollow, and within its shelter lived an old Vulture, named Grey-pate, whose hard fortune it was to have lost both eyes and talons. The birds that roosted in the tree made subscriptions from their own store, out of sheer pity for the poor fellow, and by that means he managed to live. One day, when the old birds were gone, Long-ear, the Cat, came there to get a meal of the nestlings; and they, alarmed at perceiving him, set up a chirruping that roused Grey-pate.

"Who comes there?" croaked Grey-pate.

'Now Long-ear, on espying the Vulture, thought himself undone; but as flight was impossible, he resolved to trust his destiny, and approach.

"My lord," said he, "I have the honour to salute thee."

"Who is it?" said the Vulture.

"I am a Cat."

"Be off, Cat, or I shall slay thee," said the Vulture.

"I am ready to die if I deserve death," answered the Cat; "but let what I have to say be heard."

"Wherefore, then, comest thou?" said the Vulture.

"I live," began Long-ear, "on the Ganges, bathing, and eating no flesh, practising the moon-penance ([25]), like a Bramacharya (26). The birds that resort hither constantly praise your worship to me as one wholly given to the study of morality, and worthy of all trust; and so I came here to learn law from thee, Sir, who art so deep gone in learning and in years. Dost thou, then, so read

the law of strangers as to be ready to slay a guest? What say the books about the householder?—

"Bar thy door not to the stranger, be he friend or be he foe,
For the tree will shade the woodman while his axe doth lay it low."

And, if means fail, what there is should be given with kind words; as—

"Greeting fair, and room to rest; fire, and water from the well—
Simple gifts—are given freely in the house where good men dwell,"—

and without respect of person—

"Young, or bent with many winters; rich, or poor, whate'er thy guest,
Honour him for thine own honour—better is he than the best."

Else comes the rebuke—

"Pity them that ask thy pity: who art thou to stint thy hoard,
When the holy moon shines equal on the leper and the lord!"

And that other, too,

"When thy gate is roughly fastened, and the asker turns away,
Thence he bears thy good deeds with him, and his sins on thee doth lay."

For verily,

"In the house the husband ruleth; men the Brahman 'teacher' call;
([27]) Agni is the Twice-born's Master—but the guest is lord of all."

'To these weighty words Grey-pate answered,

"Yes! but cats like meat, and there are young birds here, and therefore I said, go."

"Sir," said the Cat (and as he spoke he touched the ground, and then his two ears, and called on Krishna ([28]) to witness to his words), "I that have overcome passion, and practised the moon-penance, know the Scriptures; and howsoever they contend, in this primal duty of abstaining from injury they are unanimous. Which of them sayeth not,—

"He who does and thinks no wrong—
He who suffers, being strong—
He whose harmlessness men know—
Unto Swarga such doth go ([29])."

"I AM FAST IN THE NET."

'And so, winning the old Vulture's confidence, Long-ear, the Cat, entered the hollow tree and lived there. And day after day he stole away some of the nestlings, and brought them down to the hollow to devour. Meantime the parent birds, whose little ones were being eaten, made an inquiry after them in all quarters; and the Cat, discovering this fact, slipped out from the hollow, and made his escape. Afterwards, when the birds came to look closely, they found the bones of their young ones in the hollow of the tree where Grey-pate lived; and the birds at once concluded that their nestlings had been killed and eaten by the old Vulture, whom they accordingly executed. That is my story, and why I warned you against unknown acquaintances.'

"Sir," said the Jackal, with some warmth, "on the first day of your encountering the Deer you also were of unknown family and character: how is it, then, that your friendship with him grows daily greater? True, I am only Small-wit, the Jackal, but what says the saw?—

"In the land where no wise men are, men of little wit are lords;
And the castor-oil's a tree, if no tree else its shade affords (30)."

The Deer is my friend; condescend, sir, to be my friend also."

"Oh!" broke in the Deer, "why so much talking? We'll all live together, and be friendly and happy,—

"Foe is friend, and friend is foe,
As their actions make them so."

"Very good," said Sharp-sense; "as you will;" and in the morning each started early for his own feeding-ground (returning at night). One day the Jackal drew the Deer aside, and whispered, "Deer, in one corner of this wood there is a field full of sweet young bajri; come and let me show you." The Deer accompanied him, and found the field, and afterwards went every day there to eat the green corn, till at last the owner of the ground spied him and set a snare. The Deer came again very shortly, and was caught in it, and (after vainly struggling) exclaimed, "I am fast in the net, and it will be a net of death to me if no friend comes to rescue me!" Presently Small-wit, the Jackal, who had been lurking near, made his appearance, and standing still, he said to himself, with a chuckle, "O ho! my scheme bears fruit! When he is cut up, his bones, and gristle, and blood will fall to my share and make me some beautiful dinners." The Deer, here catching sight of him, exclaimed with rapture, "Ah, friend, this is excellent! Do but gnaw these strings, and I shall be at liberty. How charming to realize the saying!—

"That friend only is the true friend who is near when trouble comes;
That man only is the brave man who can bear the battle-drums;
Words are wind; deed proveth promise: he who helps at need is kin;
And the leal wife is loving though the husband lose or win."

And is it not written—

"Friend and kinsman—more their meaning than the idle-hearted mind.
Many a friend can prove unfriendly, many a kinsman less than kind:
He who shares his comrade's portion, be he beggar, be he lord,
Comes as truly, comes as duly, to the battle as the board—
Stands before the king to succour, follows to the pile to sigh—
He is friend, and he is kinsman—less would make the name lie."

'Small-wit answered nothing, but betook himself to examining the snare very closely.

"This will certainly hold," muttered he; then, turning to the Deer, he said, "Good friend, these strings, you see, are made of sinew, and to-day is a fast-day, so that I cannot possibly bite them. To-morrow morning, if you still desire it, I shall be happy to serve you."

When he was gone, the Crow, who had missed the Deer upon returning that evening, and had sought for him everywhere, discovered him; and seeing his sad plight, exclaimed,—

"How came this about, my friend?"

"This came," replied the Deer, "through disregarding a friend's advice."

"Where is that rascal Small-wit?" asked the Crow.

"He is waiting somewhere by," said the Deer, "to taste my flesh."

"Well," sighed the Crow, "I warned you; but it is as in the true verse,—

> "Stars gleam, lamps flicker, friends foretell of fate;
> The fated sees, knows, hears them—all too late."

And then, with a deeper sigh, he exclaimed, "Ah, traitor Jackal, what an ill deed hast thou done! Smooth-tongued knave—alas!—and in the face of the monition too,—

> "Absent, flatterers' tongues are daggers—present, softer than the silk;
> Shun them! 'tis a jar of poison hidden under harmless milk;
> Shun them when they promise little! Shun them when they promise much!
> For, enkindled, charcoal burneth—cold, it doth defile the touch."

'When the day broke, the Crow (who was still there) saw the master of the field approaching with his club in his hand.

"Now, friend Deer," said Sharp-sense on perceiving him, "do thou cause thyself to seem like one dead: puff thy belly up with wind, stiffen thy legs out, and lie very still. I will make a show of pecking thine eyes out with my beak; and whensoever I utter a croak, then spring to thy feet and betake thee to flight."

'The Deer thereon placed himself exactly as the Crow suggested, and was very soon espied by the husbandman, whose eyes opened with joy at the sight.

"Aha!" said he, "the fellow has died of himself," and so speaking, he released the Deer from the snare, and proceeded to gather and lay aside his nets. At that instant Sharp-sense uttered a loud croak, and the Deer sprang up and made off. And the club which the husbandman flung after him in a rage, struck Small-wit, the Jackal (who was close by), and killed him. Is it not said, indeed?—

> "In years, or moons, or half-moons three,
> Or in three days—suddenly,
> The knaves are shent—true men go free."

'Thou seest, then,' said Golden-skin, 'there can be no friendship between food and feeder.'

'I should hardly,' replied the Crow, 'get a large breakfast out of your worship; but as to that indeed you have nothing to fear from me. I am not often angry, and if I were, you know—

> "Anger comes to noble natures, but leaves there no strife or storm:
> Plunge a lighted torch beneath it, and the ocean grows not warm."

'Then, also, thou art such a gad-about,' objected the King.

'May-be,' answered Light o' Leap; 'but I am bent on

winning thy friendship, and I will die at thy door of fasting if thou grantest it not. Let us be friends! for

"Noble hearts are golden vases—close the bond true metals make;
Easily the smith may weld them, harder far it is to break.
Evil hearts are earthen vessels—at a touch they crack a-twain,
And what craftsman's ready cunning can unite the shards again?"

And then, too,

"Good men's friendships may be broken, yet abide they friends at heart;
Snap the stem of Luxmee's lotus, and its fibres will not part."

'Fair sir,' said the King of the Mice, 'your conversation is as pleasing as pearl necklets or oil of sandal-wood ([31]) in hot weather. Be it as you will,'—and thereon King Golden-skin made a treaty with the Crow, and after gratifying him with the best of his store re-entered his hole. The Crow returned to his accustomed perch:—and thenceforward the time passed in mutual presents of food, in polite inquiries, and the most unrestrained talk. One day Light o' Leap thus accosted Golden-skin:—

'This is a poor place, your Majesty, for a Crow to get a living in. I should like to leave it and go elsewhere.'

'Whither wouldst thou go?' replied the King; they say,

"One foot goes, and one foot stands,
When the wise man leaves his lands."

'And they say, too,' answered the Crow,

"Over-love of home were weakness; wheresoe'er the hero come,
Stalwart arm and steadfast spirit find or win for him a home.
Little recks the awless lion where his hunting jungles lie—
When he enters it be certain that a royal prey shall die."

'I know an excellent jungle now.'

'Which is that?' asked the Mouse-king.

'In the Nerbudda woods, by Camphor-water,' replied the Crow. 'There is an old and valued friend of mine lives there,—Slow-toes his name is, a very virtuous Tortoise; he will regale me with fish and good things.'

'Why should I stay behind,' said Golden-skin, 'if thou goest? Take me also.'

Accordingly, the two set forth together enjoying charming converse upon the road. Slow-toes perceived Light

o' Leap a long way off, and hastened to do him the guest-rites, extending them to the Mouse upon Light o' Leap's introduction.

'Good Slow-toes,' said he, 'this is Golden-skin, King of the Mice,—pay all honour to him,—he is burdened with virtues—a very jewel-mine of kindnesses. I don't know if the Prince of all the Serpents (32), with his two thousand tongues, could rightly repeat them.' So speaking, he told the story of Speckle-neck. Thereupon Slow-toes made a profound obeisance to Golden-skin, and said, 'How came your Majesty, may I ask, to retire to an unfrequented forest?'

'I will tell you,' said the King. 'You must know that in the town of Champaka there is a college for the devotees. Unto this resorted daily a beggar-priest, named Chudakarna, whose custom was to place his begging-dish upon the shelf, with such alms in it as he had not eaten, and go to sleep by it; and I, so soon as he slept, used to jump up, and devour the meal. One day a great friend or his, named Vinakarna, also a mendicant, came to visit him; and observed that while conversing, he kept striking the ground with a split cane, to frighten me. "Why don't you listen?" said Vinakarna. "I am listening!" replied the other; "but this plaguy mouse is always eating the meal out of my begging-dish." Vinakarna looked at the shelf and remarked, "However can a mouse jump as high as this? There must be a reason, though there seems none. I guess the cause,—the fellow is well off and fat." With these words Vinakarna snatched up a shovel, discovered my retreat, and took away all my hoard of provisions. After that I lost strength daily, had scarcely energy enough to get my dinner, and, in fact, crept about so wretchedly, that when Chudakarna saw me he fell to quoting,—

"Very féeble folk are poor folk; money lost takes wit away:
All their doings fail like runnels, wasting through the summer day."

"Yes!" I thought, "he is right, and so are the sayings—

"Wealth is friends, home, father, brother—title to respect and fame;
Yea, and wealth is held for wisdom—that it should be so is shame."

"Home is empty to the childless; hearts to them who friends deplore:
Earth unto the idle-minded; and the three worlds to the poor."

"I can stay here no longer; and to tell my distress to another is out of the question—altogether out of the question!—

"Say the sages, nine things name not: Age, domestic joys and woes,
Counsel, sickness, shame, alms, penance; neither poverty disclose.
Better for the proud of spirit, death, than life with losses told;
Fire consents to be extinguished, but submits not to be cold."

"Verily he was wise, methought also, who wrote—

"As Age doth banish beauty,
As moonlight dies in gloom,
As Slavery's menial duty
Is Honour's certain tomb;
As Hari's name and Hara's (33)
Spoken, charm sin away,
So Poverty can surely
A hundred virtues slay."

"And as to sustaining myself on another man's bread, that," I mused, "would be but a second door of death. Say not the books the same?—

"Half-known knowledge, present pleasure purchased with a future woe,
And to taste the salt of service (34)—greater griefs no man can know."

"And herein, also—

"All existence is not equal, and all living is not life;
Sick men live; and he who, banished, pines for children, home, and wife;
And the craven-hearted eater of another's leavings lives,
And the wretched captive waiting for the word of doom survives;
But they bear an anguished body, and they draw a deadly breath,
And life cometh to them only on the happy day of death."

Yet, after all these reflections, I was covetous enough to make one more attempt on Chudakarna's meal, and got a blow from the split cane for my pains. "Just so," I said to myself, "the soul and organs of the discontented want keeping in subjection. I must be done with discontent:—

"Golden gift, serene Contentment! have thou that, and all is had;
Thrust thy slipper on, and think thee that the earth is leather-clad."

"All is known, digested, tested; nothing new is left to learn
When the soul, serene, reliant, Hope's delusive dreams can spurn."

"And the sorry task of seeking favour is numbered in the miseries of life—

"Hast thou never watched, a-waiting till the great man's door unbarred?
Didst thou never linger parting, saying many a sad last word?
Spak'st thou never word of folly, one light thing thou would'st recall?
Rare and noble hath thy life been! fair thy fortune did befall!"

"No!" exclaimed I, "I will do none of these; but, by retiring into the quiet and untrodden forest, I will show my discernment of real good and ill. The holy Books counsel it—

"True Religion!—'tis not blindly prating what the priest may prate,
But to love, as God hath loved them, all things, be they small or great;
And true bliss is when a sane mind doth a healthy body fill;
And true knowledge is the knowing what is good and what is ill."

'So came I to the forest, where, by good fortune and this true friend, I met much kindness; and by the same good fortune have encountered you, Sir, whose friendliness is as Heaven to me. Ah! Sir Tortoise,

"Poisonous though the tree of life be, two fair blossoms grow thereon:
One, the company of good men; and sweet songs of Poets, one."

'King!' said Slow-toes, 'your error was getting too much, without giving. Give, says the sage—

"Give, and it shall swell thy getting; give, and thou shalt safer keep:
Pierce the tank-wall; or it yieldeth, when the water waxes deep."

And he is very hard upon money-grubbing: as thus—

"When the miser hides his treasure in the earth, he doeth well;
For he opens up a passage that his soul may sink to hell."

And thus—

"He whose coins are kept for counting, not to barter nor to give,
Breathe he like a blacksmith's bellows (35), yet in truth he doth not live."

It hath been well written, indeed,

"Gifts, bestowed with words of kindness, making giving doubly dear;
Wisdom, deep, complete, benignant, of all arrogancy clear;
Valour, never yet forgetful of sweet Mercy's pleading prayer;
Wealth, and scorn of wealth to spend it—oh! but these be virtues rare!"

'Frugal one *may* be,' continued Slow-toes; 'but not a niggard like the Jackal—

"The Jackal-knave, that starved his spirit so,
And died of saving, by a broken bow."

'Did he, indeed,' said Golden-skin; 'and how was that?'

'I will tell you,' answered Slow-toes:—

"THE BOW SPRANG BACK, AND RESOLVED HOWL O' NIGHTS INTO

The Story of the Dead Game and the Jackal.

'IN a town called "Well-to-Dwell" there lived a mighty hunter, whose name was "Grim-face." Feeling a desire one day for a little venison, he took his bow, and went into the woods; where he soon killed a deer. As he was carrying the deer home, he came upon a wild boar of prodigious proportions. Laying the deer upon the earth, he fixed and discharged an arrow and struck the boar, which instantly rushed upon him with a roar louder than the last thunder (36), and ripped the hunter up. He fell like a tree cut by the axe, and lay dead along with the boar, and a snake also, which had been crushed by the feet of the combatants. Not long afterwards, there came that way, in his prowl for food, a Jackal, named "Howl o' Nights," and cast eyes on the hunter, the deer, the boar, and the snake lying dead together. "Aha!" said he, "what luck! Here's a grand dinner got ready for me! Good fortune can come, I see, as well as ill fortune. Let me think:—the man will be fine pickings for a month; the deer with the boar will last two more; the snake will do for to-morrow; and, as I am very particularly hungry, I will treat myself now to this bit of stinking gut on the bow-horn." So saying, he began to gnaw it asunder, and the bow-string slipping, the bow sprang back, and resolved Howl o' Nights into the five elements (37) by death. That is my story,' continued Slow-toes, 'and its application is for the wise:—

"Sentences of studied wisdom, nought avail they unapplied;
Though the blind man hold a lantern, yet his footsteps stray aside."

The secret of success, indeed, is a free, contented, and yet enterprising mind. How say the books thereon?—

"Wouldst thou know whose happy dwelling Fortune entereth unknown?
His, who careless of her favour, standeth fearless in his own;
His, who for the vague to-morrow barters not the sure to-day—
Master of himself, and sternly steadfast to the rightful way;
Very mindful of past service, valiant, faithful, true of heart—
Unto such comes Lakshmi (38) smiling—comes, and will not lightly part."

What indeed,' continued Slow-toes, 'is wealth, that we should prize it, or grieve to lose it?—

"Be not haughty, being wealthy; droop not, having lost thine all;
Fate doth play with mortal fortunes as a girl doth toss her ball."

It is unstable by nature. We are told—

"Worldly friendships, fair but fleeting, shadows of the clouds at noon,
Women (39), youth, new corn, and riches—these be pleasures passing soon."

And it is idle to be anxious; the Master of Life knows how to sustain it. Is it not written?—

"For thy bread be not o'er thoughtful—God for all hath taken thought:
When the babe is born, the sweet milk to the mother's breast is brought.

He who gave the swan her silver, and the hawk her plumes of pride,
And his purples to the peacock—He will verily provide."

Yes, verily,' said Slow-toes, 'wealth is bad to handle, and better left alone; there is no truer saying than this—

"Though for good ends, waste not on wealth a minute ;
Mud may be wiped, but wise men plunge not in it."

Hearing the wisdom of these monitions, Light o' Leap broke out, "Good Slow-toes! thou art a wise protector of those that come to thee; thy learning comforts my enlightened friend, as elephants drag elephants from the mire." And thus, on the best of terms, wandering where they pleased for food, the three lived there together.

One day it chanced that a Deer named Dapple-back ([40]), who had seen some cause of alarm in the forest, came suddenly upon the three in his flight. Thinking the danger imminent, Slow-toes dropped into the water, King Golden-skin slipped into his hole, and Light o' Leap flew up into the top of a high tree. Thence he looked all round to a great distance, but could discover nothing. So they all came back again, and sat down together. Slow-toes welcomed the Deer.

"Good Deer," said he, "may grass and water never fail thee at thy need. Gratify us by residing here, and consider this forest thine own."

"Indeed," answered Dapple-back, "I came hither for your protection, flying from a hunter; and to live with you in friendship is my greatest desire."

"Then the thing is settled," observed Golden-skin.

"Yes! yes!" said Light o' Leap, "make yourself altogether at home!"

So the Deer, charmed at his reception, eat grass and drank water, and laid himself down in the shade of a Banyan-tree to talk. Who does not know?—

"Brunettes, and the Banyan's shadow,
Well-springs, and a brick-built wall,
Are all alike cool in the summer,
And warm in the winter—all."

"What made thee alarmed, friend Deer?" began Slow-toes: "Do hunters ever come to this unfrequented forest?"

"I *have* heard," replied Dapple-back, "that the Prince of the Kalinga country, Rukmangada, is coming here. He is even now encamped on the Cheenab River, on his march to subjugate the borders; and the hunters have been heard to say that he will halt to-morrow by this very lake of 'Camphor-water.' Don't you think, as it is dangerous to stay, that we ought to resolve on something?"

"*I* shall certainly go to another pool," exclaimed Slow-toes.

"It would be better," answered the Crow and Deer together.

"Yes!" remarked the King of the Mice, after a minute's thought; "but how is Slow-toes to get across the country in time? Animals like our amphibious host are best in the water; on land he might suffer from his own design, like the merchant's son—

"The merchant's son laid plans for gains,
And saw his wife kissed for his pains."

"How came that about?" asked all.

"I'll tell you," answered Golden-skin.

The Prince and the Wife of the Merchant's Son.

'IN the country of Kanouj there was a King named Virasena, and he made his son viceroy of a city called Virapoora. The Prince was rich, handsome, and in the bloom of youth. Passing through the streets of his city one day, he observed a very lovely woman, whose name was Lávanyavati—*i.e.*, the Beautiful—the wife of a merchant's son. On reaching his palace, full of her charms and of passionate admiration for them, he despatched a message to her, and a letter, by a female attendant :—who wonders at it ?—

"Ah ! the gleaming, glancing arrows of a lovely woman's eye !
Feathered with her jetty lashes, perilous they pass us by :
Loosed at venture from the black bows of her arching brow they part,
All too penetrant and deadly for an undefended heart."

Now Lávanyavati, from the moment she saw the Prince, was hit with the same weapon of love that wounded him ; but upon hearing the message of the attendant, she refused with dignity to receive his letter.

"I am my husband's," she said, "and that is my honour ; for—

"Beautiful the Koïl (11) seemeth for the sweetness of his song,
Beautiful the world esteemeth pious souls for patience strong ;
Homely features lack not favour when true wisdom they reveal,
And a wife is fair and honoured while her heart is firm and leal."

What the lord of my life enjoins, that I do."

"Is such my answer?" asked the attendant.

"It is," said Lávanyavati.

Upon the messenger reporting her reply to the Prince, he was in despair.

"The God of the five shafts ([42]) has hit me," he exclaimed, "and only her presence will cure my wound."

"We must make her husband bring her, then," said the messenger.

"That can never be," replied the Prince.

"It can," replied the messenger,—

> "Fraud may achieve what force would never try:
> The Jackal killed the Elephant thereby."

"How was that?" asked the Prince.

The Slave related:—

The Story of the Old Jackal and the Elephant.

"IN the forest of Brahma ([43]) lived an Elephant, whose name was 'White-front.' The Jackals knew him, and said among themselves, 'If this great brute would but die, there would be four months' food for us, and plenty, out of his carcase.' With that an old Jackal stood up, and pledged himself to compass the death of the Elephant by his own wit. Accordingly, he sought for 'White-front,' and, going up to him, he made the reverential prostration of the eight members ([44]), gravely saluting him.

"PERHAPS YOUR MAJESTY," SAID THE JACKAL, WITH AN IMPUDENT LAUGH, "WILL CONDESCEND TO TAKE HOLD OF THE TIP OF MY BRUSH."

'Divine creature,' said he, 'vouchsafe me the regard of one look.'

'Who art thou?' grunted the Elephant, 'and whence comest thou?'

'I am only a Jackal,' said the other; 'but the beasts of the forest are convinced that it is not expedient to live without a king, and they have met in full council, and despatched me to acquaint your Royal Highness that on you, endowed with so many lordly qualities, their choice has fallen for a sovereign over the forest here; for—

> "Who is just, and strong, and wise?
> Who is true to social ties?
> He is formed for Emperies."

Let your Majesty, therefore, repair thither at once, that the moment of fortunate conjunction ([15]) may not escape us.' So saying he led the way, followed at a great pace by White-front who was eager to commence his reign.

"Presently the Jackal brought him upon a deep slough, into which he plunged heavily before he could stop himself.

'Good master Jackal,' cried the Elephant, 'what's to do now? I am up to my belly in this quagmire.'

'Perhaps your Majesty,' said the Jackal, with an impudent laugh, 'will condescend to take hold of the tip of my brush with your trunk, and so get out.'

"Then White-front, the Elephant, knew that he had been deceived; and thus he sank in the slime, and was devoured by the Jackals. Hence," continued the attendant, "is why I suggested stratagem to your highness."

Shortly afterwards, by the Slave's advice, the Prince

sent for the merchant's son (whose name was Charu-datta), and appointed him to be near his person; and one day, with the same design, when he was just come from the bath, and had on his jewels, he summoned Charudatta, and said,—

"I have a vow to keep to Gauri (46)—bring hither to me every evening for a month some lady of good family, that

I may do honour to her, according to my vow; and begin to-day."

Charudatta in due course brought a lady of quality, and, having introduced her, retired to watch the interview. The Prince, without even approaching his fair visitor, made her the most respectful obeisances, and dismissed her with gifts of ornaments, sandal-wood, and perfumes, under the protection of a guard. This made Charudatta confident, and longing to get some of these princely presents he brought his own wife next evening.

When the Prince recognized the charming Lávanyavati—the joy of his soul—he sprang to meet her, and kissed and caressed her without the least restraint. At sight of this the miserable Charudatta stood transfixed with despair—the very picture of wretchedness '——

"And you too, Slow-toes—but where is he gone?" abruptly asked King Golden-skin.

Now Slow-toes had not chosen to wait the end of the story, but was gone before, and Golden-skin and the others followed him up in some anxiety. The Tortoise had been painfully travelling along, until a hunter, who was beating the wood for game, had overtaken him. The fellow, who was very hungry, picked him up, fastened him on his bow-stick, and set off for home; while the Deer, the Crow, and the Mouse, who had witnessed the capture, followed them in dreadful concern. "Alas!" cried the Mouse-king, "he is gone!—and such a friend!

> "Friend! gracious word!—the heart to tell is ill able
> Whence came to men this jewel of a syllable."

"Let us," continued he to his companions, "let us make one attempt, at least, to rescue Slow-toes before the hunter is out of the wood!"

"Only tell us how to do it," replied they.

"Do thus," said Golden-skin: "let Dapple-back hasten on to the water, and lie down there and make himself appear dead; and do you, Light o' Leap, hover over him and peck about his body. The hunter is sure to put the Tortoise down to get the venison, and I will gnaw his bonds."

'The Deer and the Crow started at once; and the hunter, who was sitting down to rest under a tree and drinking water, soon caught sight of the Deer, apparently dead. Drawing his wood-knife, and putting the Tortoise down by the water, he hastened to secure the Deer, and Golden-skin, in the meantime, gnawed asunder the string that held Slow-toes, who instantly dropped into the pool. The Deer, of course, when the hunter got near, sprang up and made off, and when he returned to the tree the Tortoise was gone also. "I deserve this," thought he—

"Whoso for greater quits his gain,
Shall have his labour for his pain;
The things unwon unwon remain,
And what was won is lost again."

And so lamenting, he went to his village. Slow-toes and his friends, quit of all fears, repaired together to their new habitations, and there lived happily.

Then spake the King Sudarsana's sons, "We have heard every word, and are delighted; it fell out just as we wished."

"I rejoice thereat, my Princes," said Vishnu-Sarman; "may it also fall out according to this my wish—

"Lakshmi give you friends like these!
Lakshmi keep your lands in ease!
Set, your sovereign thrones beside,
Policy, a winsome bride!
And He, whose forehead-jewel is the moon ([17])
Give peace to us and all—serene and soon."

The Parting of Friends.

THEN spake the Royal Princes to Vishnu-Sarman, "Reverend Sir! we have listened to the 'Winning of Friends,' we would now hear how friends are parted."

"Attend, then," replied the Sage, "to 'the Parting of Friends,' the first couplet of which runs in this wise—

"The Jackal set—of knavish cunning full—
At loggerheads the Lion and the Bull."

"How was that?" asked the sons of the Rajah.

Vishnu-Sarman proceeded to relate:—

The Story of the Lion, the Jackals, and the Bull.

"IN the Deccan there is a city called Golden-town, and a wealthy merchant lived there named Well-to-do. He had abundant means, but as many of his relations were even yet richer, his mind was bent upon outdoing them by gaining more. Enough is never what we have—

"Looking down on lives below them, men of little store are great;
Looking up to higher fortunes, hard to each man seems his fate."

And is not wealth won by courage and enterprise?—

"As a bride, unwisely wedded, shuns the cold caress of eld,
So, from coward souls and slothful, Lakshmi's favours turn repelled."

"Ease, ill-health, home-keeping, sleeping, woman-service, and content—
In the path that leads to greatness these be six obstructions sent."

And wealth that increases not, diminishes—a little gain is so far good—

"Seeing how the soorma (48) wasteth, seeing how the ant-hill grows (49),
Little adding unto little—live, give, learn, as life-time goes."

"Drops of water falling, falling, falling, brim the chatty (50) o'er;
Wisdom comes in little lessons—little gains make largest store."

Moved by these reflections Well-to-do loaded a cart with wares of all kinds, yoked two bulls to it, named Lusty-life and Roarer, and started for Kashmir to trade. He had not gone far upon his journey when in passing through a great forest called Bramble-wood, Lusty-life slipped down and broke his foreleg. At sight of this disaster Well-to-do fell a thinking, and repeated,—

"Men their cunning schemes may spin—
God knows who shall lose or win."

Comforting himself with such philosophy, Well-to-do left Lusty-life there, and went on his way. The Bull watched him depart, and stood mournfully on three legs, alone in the forest. 'Well, well,' he thought, 'it is all destiny whether I live or die:—

"Shoot a hundred shafts, the quarry lives and flies—not due to death;
When his hour is come, a grass-blade hath a point to stop his breath."

As the days passed by, and Lusty-life picked about in the tender forest grass, he grew wonderfully well, and fat of carcase, and happy, and bellowed about the wood as

though it were his own. Now, the reigning monarch of the forest was King Tawny-hide the Lion, who ruled over the whole country absolutely, by right of having deposed everybody else. Is not might right?—

"Robes were none, nor oil of unction, when the King of Beasts was crowned:
'Twas his own fierce roar proclaimed him, rolling all his kingdom round."

One morning, his Majesty, being exceedingly thirsty, had repaired to the bank of the Jumna to drink water, and just as he was about to lap it, the bellow of Lusty-life, awful as the thunder of the last day, reached the imperial ears. Upon catching the sound the king retreated in trepidation to his own lair, without drinking a drop, and stood there in silence and alarm, revolving what it could mean. In this position he was observed by the sons of his minister, two jackals named Karataka and Damanaka, who began to remark upon it.

'Friend Karataka,' said the last, 'what makes our royal master slink away from the river when he was dying to drink?'

'Why should we care?' replied Karataka. 'It's bad enough to serve him, and be neglected for our pains,—

"Oh, the bitter salt of service!—toil, frost, fire, are not so keen:
Half such heavy penance bearing, tender consciences were clean."

'Nay, friend! never think thus,' said Damanaka,—

"What but for their vassals,
 Elephant and man—
Swing of golden tassels,
 Wave of silken fan—
But for regal manner
 That the 'Chattra' ([51]) brings,
Horse, and foot, and banner—
 What would come of kings?"

'I care not,' replied Karataka; 'we have nothing to do with it, and matters that don't concern us are best left alone. You know the story of the Monkey, don't you?—

"HE BEGAN TO TUG AT THE WEDGE."

"The Monkey drew the sawyer's wedge, and died:
Let meddlers mark it, and be edified."

'No!' said Damanaka. 'How was it?'

'In this way,' answered Karataka:—

The Story of the Monkey and the Wedge.

'IN South Behar, close by the retreat of Dharmma (52), there was an open plot of ground, upon which a temple was in course of erection, under the management of a man of the Káyeth caste (53), named Subhadatta. A carpenter upon the works had partly sawed through a long beam of wood, and wedged it open, and was gone away, leaving the wedge fixed. Shortly afterwards a large herd of monkeys came frolicking that way, and one of their number, directed doubtless by the Angel of death, got astride the beam, and grasped the wedge, with his tail and lower parts dangling down between the pieces of the wood. Not content with this, in the mischief natural to monkeys, he began to tug at the wedge; till at last it yielded to a great effort and came out; when the wood closed upon him, and jammed him all fast. So perished the monkey, miserably crushed; and I say again,—

"Let meddlers mark it, and be edified."

'But surely,' argued Damanaka, 'servants are bound to watch the movements of their masters!'

'Let the prime minister do it, then,' answered Karataka; 'it is his business to overlook things, and subordinates shouldn't interfere in the department of their chief. You might get ass's thanks for it,—

> "The Ass that hee-hawed, when the dog should do it,
> For his lord's welfare, like an ass did rue it."

Damanaka asked how that happened, and Karataka related :—

The Story of the Washerman's Jackass.

'THERE was a certain Washerman ([54]) at Benares, whose name was Carpúrapataka, and he had an Ass and a Dog in his courtyard; the first tethered, and the last roaming loose. Once on a time, when he had been spending his morning in the society of his wife, whom he had just married, and had fallen to sleep in her arms, a robber entered the house, and began to carry off his goods. The Ass observed the occupation of the thief, and was much concerned.

"Good Dog," said he, "this is thy matter: why dost thou not bark aloud, and rouse the master?"

"Gossip Ass," replied the Dog, "leave me alone to guard the premises. I can do it, if I choose; but the truth is, this master of ours thinks himself so safe lately that he clean forgets me, and I don't find my allowance of food nearly regular enough. Masters will do so; and a little fright will put him in mind of his defenders again."

"Thou scurvy cur!" exclaimed the Ass—

"At the work-time, asking wages—is it like a faithful herd?"

"Thou extreme Ass!" replied the Dog.

"When the work's done, grudging wages—is *that* acting like a lord?"

"Mean-spirited beast," retorted the Ass, "who neglectest thy master's business! Well, then, I at least will endeavour to arouse him; it is no less than religion,

"Serve the Sun with sweat of body; starve thy maw to feed the flame (55);
Stead thy lord with all thy service; to thy death go, quit of blame."

So saying, he put forth his very best braying. The Washerman sprang up at the noise, and missing the thief, turned in a rage upon the Ass for disturbing him, and beat it with a cudgel to such an extent that the blows resolved the poor animal into the five elements of death. 'So that,' continued Karataka, 'is why I say, Let the prime minister look to him. The hunting for prey is our duty—let us stick to it, then. And this,' he said, with a meditative look, 'need not trouble us to-day; for we have a capital dish of the royal leavings.'

'What!' said Damanaka, rough with rage, 'dost thou serve the King for the sake of thy belly? Why take any such trouble to preserve an existence like thine?—

"Many prayers for him are uttered whereon many a life relies;
'Tis but one poor fool the fewer when the gulping Raven dies."

For assisting friends, and defeating enemies also, the

service of kings is desirable. To enter upon it for a mere living makes the thing low indeed. There must be dogs and elephants; but servants need not be like hungry curs, while their masters are noble. What say the books?—

> "Give thy Dog the merest mouthful, and he crouches at thy feet,
> Wags his tail, and fawns, and grovels, in his eagerness to eat;
> Bid the Elephant be feeding, and the best of fodder bring;
> Gravely—after much entreaty—condescends that mighty king."

'Well, well!' said Karataka; 'the books are nothing to us, who are not councillors.'

'But we may come to be,' replied Damanaka; 'men rise, not by chance or nature, but by exertions,—

> "By their own deeds men go downward, by them men mount upward all,
> Like the diggers of a well, and like the builders of a wall."

Advancement is slow—but that is in the nature of things,—

> "Rushes down the hill the crag, which upward 'twas so hard to roll:
> So to virtue slowly rises—so to vice quick sinks the soul."

'Very good,' observed Karataka; 'but what is all this talk about?'

'Why! don't you see our Royal Master there, and how he came home without drinking? I know he has been horribly frightened,' said Damanaka.

'How do you know it?' asked the other.

'By my perception—at a glance!' replied Damanaka; 'and I mean to make out of this occasion that which shall put his Majesty at my disposal.'

'Now,' exclaimed Karataka, 'it is thou who art ignorant about service,—

"Who speaks unasked, or comes unbid,
Or counts on favour—will be chid."

'I ignorant about service!' said Damanaka; 'no, no, my friend, I know the secret of it,—

"Wise, modest, constant, ever close at hand,
Not weighing but obeying all command,
Such servant by a Monarch's throne may stand."

'In any case, the King often rates thee,' remarked Karataka, 'for coming to the presence unsummoned.'

'A dependant,' replied Damanaka, 'should nevertheless present himself; he must make himself known to the great man, at any risk,—

"Pitiful, who fearing failure, therefore no beginning makes,
Why forswear a daily dinner for the chance of stomach-aches?"

and besides, to be near is at last to be needful;—is it not said,—

"Nearest to the King is dearest, be thy merit low or high;
Women, creeping plants, and princes, twine round that which groweth nigh."'

'Well,' inquired Karataka, 'what wilt thou say, being come to him?'

'First,' replied Damanaka, 'I will discover if his Majesty is well affected to me.'

'How do you compass that?' asked the other.

'Oh, easily! by a look, a word,' answered Damanaka; 'and that ascertained, I will proceed to speak what will put him at my disposal.'

'I can't see how you can venture to speak,' objected the other, 'without an opportunity,—

"If Vrihaspati, the Grave (56),
Spoke a sentence out of season,
Even Vrihaspati would have
Strong rebuke for such unreason."

'Pray don't imagine I shall speak unseasonably,' interrupted Damanaka; 'if that is all you fear, I will start at once.'

'Go, then,' said Karataka; 'and may you be as lucky as you hope.'

"Thereupon Damanaka set out for the lair of King Tawny-hide; putting on, as he approached it, the look of one greatly disconcerted. The Rajah observed him coming, and gave permission that he should draw near; of which Damanaka availing himself, made reverential prostration of the eight members, and sat down upon his haunches.

'You have come at last, then, Sir Jackal!' growled his Majesty.

'Great Monarch!' humbly replied Damanaka, 'my service is not worthy of laying at your imperial feet, but a servant should attend when he can perform a service, and therefore I am come,—

"When Kings' ears itch, they use a straw to scratch 'em;
When Kings' foes plot, they get wise men to match 'em."

'H'm!' growled the Lion.

'Your Majesty suspects my intellect, I fear,' continued the Jackal, 'after so long an absence from your Majesty's feet; but, if I may say so, it is still sound.'

'H'm!' growled the Lion again.

'A king, may it please your Majesty, should know how to estimate his servants, whatever their position,—

"Pearls are dull in leaden settings, but the setter is to blame;
Glass will glitter like the ruby, dulled with dust—are they the same?"

"And a fool may tread on jewels, setting in his crown mere glass;
Yet, at selling, gems are gems, and fardels but for fardels pass."

'Servants, gracious liege! are good or bad as they are entertained. Is it not written?—

"Horse and weapon, lute and volume, man and woman, gift of speech,
Have their uselessness or uses in the One who owneth each."

'And if I have been traduced to your Majesty as a dull fellow, that hath not made me so,—

"Not disparagement nor slander kills the spirit of the brave;
Fling a torch down, upward ever burns the brilliant flame it gave."

'Accept then, Sire, from the humblest of your slaves his very humble counsel—for

"Wisdom from the mouth of children be it overpast of none;
What man scorns to walk by lamplight in the absence of the sun?"

'Good Damanaka,' said King Tawny-hide, somewhat appeased, 'how is it that thou, so wise a son of our first minister, hast been absent all this while from our Court? But now speak thy mind fearlessly: what wouldst thou?'

'Will your Majesty deign to answer one question?' said Damanaka. 'Wherefore came He back from the river without drinking?'

'Hush!' whispered the King, 'thou hast hit right upon my trouble. I knew no one unto whom I might confide it; but thou seemest a faithful fellow, and I will tell thee. Listen, then,' continued his Majesty in an agitated whisper, 'there is some awful beast that was never seen before in this wood here; and we shall have to leave it, look you. Did you hear by chance the inconceivable great roar he gave? What a strong beast it must be to have such a voice!'

'May it please your Majesty, I *did* hear the noise,' said the Jackal, 'and there is doubtless cause for terrible apprehension therein; but take comfort, my liege, he is no minister who bids thee prepare for either war or resignation. All will go well, and your Majesty will learn by this difficulty which be your best servants.'

'Good Jackal,' said Tawny-hide, 'I am horribly frightened about it.'

'I can see that,' thought Damanaka; but he only said, 'Fear nothing, my liege, while thy servant survives.'

'What shall I do?' asked the King.

'It is well to encourage those who can avert disaster. If your Majesty condescended now to bestow some favour on Karataka and the other——'

'It shall be done,' said the Rajah; and, summoning the other Jackals, he gave them and Damanaka a magnificent gift of flesh, and they left the presence, undertaking to meet the threatened danger.

'But, brother,' began Karataka, 'haven't we eaten the King's dinner without knowing what the danger is which we are to meet, and whether we can obviate it?'

'Hold thy peace,' said Damanaka, laughing; 'I know very well what the danger is! It was a bull, aha! that bellowed—a bull, my brother—whose beef you and I could pick, much more the King our master.'

'And why not tell him so?' asked Karataka.

'What! and quiet his Majesty's fears! And where would our splendid dinner have been then? No, no, my friend,—

"Set not your lord at ease; for, doing that,
Might starve you as it starved 'Curd-ear' the Cat."

'Who was Curd-ear, the Cat?' inquired Karataka. Damanaka related:—

The Story of the Cat who served the Lion.

'FAR away in the North (37), on a mountain named "Thousand-Crags," there lived a lion called "Mighty-heart;" and he was much annoyed by a certain mouse, who made a custom of nibbling his mane while he lay asleep in his den. The Lion would wake in a great rage at finding the ends of his magnificent mane made ragged, but the little mouse ran into his hole, and he could never catch it. After much consideration he went down to a village, and got a Cat named Curd-ear to come to his cave with much persuasion. He kept the Cat royally on all kinds of dainties, and slept comfortably without having his mane nibbled, as the mouse would now never venture out. Whenever the Lion heard the mouse scratching about, that was always a signal for regaling the Cat in a most distinguished style. But one day, the wretched mouse being nearly starved, he took courage to creep timidly from his hole, and was directly pounced upon by Curd-ear and killed. After that the Lion heard no more of the mouse, and quite left off his regular entertainments of the Cat. No!' concluded Damanaka, 'we will keep our mouse alive for his Majesty.'

"So conversing, the Jackals went away to find Lusty-life the Bull, and upon discovering him, Karataka squatted down with great dignity at the foot of a tree, while Damanaka approached to accost him.

'Bull,' said Damanaka, 'I am the warder of this forest under the King Tawny-hide, and Karataka the Jackal there is his General. The General bids thee come before him, or else instantly depart from the wood. It were better for thee to obey, for his anger is terrible.'

"Thereupon Lusty-life, knowing nothing of the country customs, advanced at once to Karataka, made the respectful prostration of the eight members, and said timidly, 'My Lord General! what dost thou bid me do?—

"'Strength serves Reason. Saith the Mahout, when he beats the brazen drum,
'Ho! ye elephants, to this work must your mightinesses come.'"

'Bull,' answered Karataka, 'thou canst remain in the wood no longer unless thou goest directly to lay thyself at our Royal master's imperial feet.'

'My Lord,' replied the Bull, 'give me a guarantee of safety, and I will go.'

'Bull,' said Karataka, 'thou art foolish; fear nothing,—

"When the King of Chedi ([58]) cursed him,
Krishna scorned to make reply;
Lions roar the thunder quiet,
Jackals'-yells they let go by."

Our Lord the King will not vouchsafe his anger to thee; knowest thou not—

"Mighty natures war with mighty: when the raging tempests blow,
O'er the green rice harmless pass they, but they lay the palm-trees low."

"So the Jackals, keeping Lusty-life in the rear, went towards the palace of King Tawny-hide; where the Rajah received them with much graciousness, and bade them sit down.

'Have you seen him?' asked the King.

'We have seen him, your Majesty,' answered Damanaka; 'it is quite as your Majesty expected—the creature has enormous strength, and wishes to see your Majesty. Will you be seated, Sire, and prepare yourself—it will never do to appear alarmed at a noise.'

'Oh, if it was only a noise,' began the Rajah.

'Ah, but the cause, Sire! that was what had to be found out; like the secret of Swing-ear the Spirit.'

'And who might Swing-ear be?' asked the King.

The Story of the Terrible Bell.

'A GOBLIN, your Majesty,' responded Damanaka, 'it seemed so, at least, to the good people of Brahmapoora. A thief had stolen a bell from the city, and was making off with that plunder, and more, into the Sri-parvata hills, when he was killed by a tiger. The bell lay in the jungle till some monkeys picked it up, and amused themselves by constantly ringing it. The townspeople found the bones of the man, and heard the noise of the bell all about the hills; so they gave out that there was a terrible devil there, whose ears rang like bells as he swung them about, and whose delight was to devour men. Every one, accordingly, was leaving the town, when a peasant woman named Karála, who liked belief the better for a little proof, came to the Rajah.

"Highness!" she observed, "for a consideration I could settle this Swing-ear."

"You could!" exclaimed the Rajah.

"I think so!" repeated the woman.

"Give her a consideration forthwith," said the Rajah.

'Karála, who had her own ideas upon the matter, took the present and set out. Being come to the hills, she made a circle, and did homage to Gunputtee ([38]), without whom nothing prospers. Then, taking some fruit she had brought, such as monkeys love extremely, she scattered it up and down in the wood, and withdrew to watch. Very soon the monkeys finding the fruit, put down the bell, to do justice to it, and the woman picking it up, bore it back to the town, where she became an object of uncommon veneration. We, indeed,' concluded Damanaka, 'bring you a Bull instead of a bell--your Majesty shall now see him!'

"Thereupon Lusty-life was introduced, and, the interview passing off well, he remained many days in the forest on excellent terms with the Lion.

"One day another Lion, named 'Stiff-ears,' the brother of King Tawny-hide, came to visit him. The King received him with all imaginable respect, bade him be seated, and rose from his throne to go and kill some beasts for his refreshment.

'May it please your Majesty,' interposed the Bull, 'a deer was slain to-day—where is its flesh?'

'Damanaka and his brother know best,' said the King.

'Let us ascertain if there be any,' suggested the Bull.

'It is useless,' said the King, laughing,—'they leave none.'

'What!' exclaimed the Bull, 'have those Jackals eaten a whole deer?'

'Eaten it, spoiled it, and given it away,' answered Tawny-hide; 'they always do so.'

'And this without your Majesty's sanction?' asked the Bull.

'Oh! certainly not with my sanction,' said the King.

'Then,' exclaimed the Bull, 'it is too bad: and in Ministers too!—

> "Narrow-necked to let out little, big of belly to keep much
> As a flagon is—the Vizier of a Sultan should be such."

'No wealth will stand such waste, your Majesty,—

> "He who thinks a minute little, like a fool misuses more;
> He who counts a cowry (60) nothing, being wealthy, will be poor."

'A king's treasury, my liege, is the king's life.'

'Good brother,' observed Stiff-ears, who had heard what the Bull said, 'these Jackals are your Ministers of Home and Foreign Affairs,—they should not have direction of the Treasury. They are old servants, too, and you know the saying,—

> "Brahmans, soldiers, these and kinsmen—of the three set none in charge:
> For the Brahman, tho' you rack him, yields no treasure small or large;
> And the soldier, being trusted, writes his quittance with his sword,
> And the kinsman cheats his kindred by the charter of the word;
> But a servant old in service, worse than any one is thought,
> Who, by long-tried licence fearless, knows his master's anger nought."

Ministers, my royal brother, are often like obstinate swellings that want squeezing, and yours must be kept in order.'

'They are not particularly obedient, I confess,' said Tawny-hide.

'It is very wrong,' replied Stiff-ears; 'and if you will be advised by me—as we have banqueted enough to-day—you will appoint this grain-eating and sagacious Bull your Superintendent of Stores.'

'It shall be so,' exclaimed the King.

"Lusty-life was accordingly appointed to serve out the provisions, and for many days Tawny-hide showed him favour beyond all others in the Court.

"Now the Jackals soon found that food was no longer

so freely provided by this arrangement as before, and they met to consult about it.

'It is all our own fault,' said Damanaka, 'and people must suffer for their own mistakes. You know who said—

> " I that could not leave alone
> 'Streak-o'-Gold,' must therefore moan.
> She that took the House-wife's place
> Lost the nose from off her face.
> Take this lesson to thy heart—
> Fools for folly suffer smart."

'No!' said Karataka, 'how was it?' Damanaka related :—

The Story of the Prince and the Procuress who suffered for their own Faults.

'IN the city of "Golden-streets" there reigned a valorous King, named Vira-vikrama, whose officer of justice was one day taking away to punishment a certain Barber, when he was stopped by a strolling mendicant, who held him by the skirts, and cried out, "Punish not this man—punish them that do wrong of their own knowledge." Being asked his meaning, he recited the foregoing verses, and, being still further questioned, he told this story—

"I am Prince Kandarpa-ketu, son of the King of Ceylon. Walking one day in my summer-garden, I heard a merchant-captain narrating how that out at sea, deep under water, on the fourteenth day of the moon, he had seen what was like nothing but the famous tree of Paradise (61), and sitting under it a lady of most lustrous beauty, bedecked with strings of pearls like Lukshmi herself, reclining, with a lute in her hands, on what appeared to be a golden couch crusted all over with precious stones. At once I engaged the captain and his ship, and steered to the spot of which he told me. On reaching it I beheld the beautiful apparition as he had described it, and, transported with the exquisite beauty of the lady, I leapt after her into the sea. In a moment I found myself in a city of gold; and in an apartment of a golden palace, surrounded by young and beautiful girls, I found the Sea-queen. She perceived my approach, and sent an attendant with a courteous message to meet me. In reply to my questions, I learned that the lady was the Princess Ratnamanjari, daughter of the King of All the Spirits—and how she had made a vow that whoever should first come to see her golden city with his own eyes should marry her. So I married her by the form called Gundharva (62), or 'Union by mutual consent,' and spent many and happy days in her delightful society. One day she took me aside, and said, 'Dear Prince! all these delights, and I myself, are thine to enjoy; only that picture yonder, of the Fairy Streak-o'-Gold, that thou must never touch!' For a long time I observed this injunction; at last, impelled by resistless curiosity, I laid my hand on the picture of 'Streak-o'-Gold.' In one instant her little foot, lovely as the lotus-blossom, advanced from out of the painting, and launched me through sea and air into my own country. Since that I have been a miserable wanderer; and passing through this city, I chanced to lodge at a

"I FOUND THE SEA QUEEN."

Cowkeeper's hut, and saw the truth of this Barber's affair. The herdsman returned at night with his cattle, and found his wife talking with the wife of the Barber, who is no better than a bawd. Enraged at this, the man beat his wife, tied her to the milking-post, and fell asleep. In the dead of the night the Barber's wife came back, and said to the woman, 'He whom thou knowest is burnt with the cruel fire of thine absence, and lies nigh to death; go therefore and console him, and I will tie myself to the post until thou returnest.' This was done, and the Cowkeeper presently awoke. 'Ah! thou light thing!' he said jeeringly, 'why dost not thou keep promise, and meet thy gallant?' The Barber's wife could make no reply; whereat becoming incensed, the man cried out, 'What! dost thou scorn to speak to me? I will cut thy nose off (63)!' And so he did, and then lay down to sleep again. Very soon the Cowkeeper's wife came back and asked if 'all was well.' 'Look at my face!' said the Barber's wife, 'and you will see if all is well.' The woman could do nothing but take her place again, while the Barber's wife, picking up the severed nose, and at a sad loss how to account for it, went to her house. In the morning, before it was light, the Barber called to her to bring his box of razors, and she bringing one only, he flung it away in a passion. 'Oh, the knave!' she cried out aloud, directly, 'Neighbours, neighbours! he has cut my nose off!' and so she took him before the officers. The Cowkeeper, meantime, wondering at his wife's patience, made some inquiry about her nose; whereto she replied, 'Cruel wretch! thou canst not harm a virtuous woman. If Yama and the seven guardians of the world (64) know me chaste, then be my face unmaimed!' The herdsman hastened to fetch a light, and finding her features unaltered, he flung himself at her feet, and begged forgiveness. For,

> "Never tires the fire of burning, never wearies death of slaying,
> Nor the sea of drinking rivers, nor the bright-eyed of betraying."

Thereupon the King's officer dismissed Kandarpa-ketu, and did justice by setting the Barber free, shaving the head of the Barber's wife ([65]), and punishing the Cow-keeper's.

'That is my story,' concluded Damanaka, 'and thence I said that we had no reason to complain.'

'Well, but we must do something,' said Karataka.

'Yes! How shall we break the friendship of the King with the Bull?' asked the other.

'It is very strong,' observed Karataka.

'But we can do it,' replied the other.

> "What force would fail to win, fraud can attain:
> The Crow despatched the Serpent by a chain."

'How did that occur?' asked Karataka.

Damanaka related:—

The Story of the Black Snake and the Golden Chain.

'A PAIR of Crows had their abode in a certain tree, the hollow of which was occupied by a black snake, who had often devoured their young. The Hen-bird, finding herself breeding again, thus addressed her mate: "Husband, we must leave this tree; we shall never rear young ones while this black snake lives here! You know the saw—

> "From false friends that breed thee strife,
> From a house with serpents rife,
> Saucy slaves and brawling wife—
> Get thee out, to save thy life."

"My dear," replied the Crow, "you need not fear; I have put up with him till I am tired. Now I will put an end to him."

"How can you fight with a great black snake like that?" said the Hen-bird.

"Doubt nothing," answered the other—

> "He that hath sense hath strength; the fool is weak:
> The Lion proud died by the Hare so meek."

"How came that about?" asked the Hen-Crow.

"Thus," replied her mate:—

The Story of the Lion and the Old Hare.

"ON the Mandara mountain there lived a Lion named Fierce-of-heart, and he was perpetually making massacre of all the wild animals. The thing grew so bad that the beasts held a public meeting, and drew up a respectful remonstrance to the Lion in these words:

'Wherefore should your Majesty thus make carnage of us all? If it may please you, we ourselves will daily furnish a beast for your Majesty's meal.' The Lion responded, 'If that arrangement is more agreeable to you, be it so;' and from that time a beast was allotted to him

daily, and daily devoured. One day it came to the turn of an old hare to supply the royal table, who reflected to himself as he walked along, 'I can but die, and I will go to my death leisurely.'

"Now Fierce-of-heart, the lion, was pinched with hunger, and seeing the Hare so approaching he roared out, 'How darest thou thus delay in coming?'

'Sire,' replied the Hare, 'I am not to blame. I was detained on the road by another lion, who exacted an oath from me to return when I should have informed your Majesty.'

'Go,' exclaimed King Fierce-of-heart in a rage; 'show me, instantly, where this insolent villain of a lion lives.'

"The Hare led the way accordingly till he came to a deep well, whereat he stopped, and said, 'Let my lord the King come hither and behold him.' The Lion approached, and beheld his own reflection in the water of the well, upon which, in his passion, he directly flung himself, and so perished."

"I have heard your story," said the Hen-Crow, "but what plan do you propose?"

"My dear," replied her mate, "the Rajah's son comes here every day to bathe in the stream. When he takes off his gold anklet, and lays it on the stone, do thou bring it in thy beak to the hollow of the tree, and drop it in there." Shortly after the Prince came, as was his wont, and taking off his dress and ornaments, the Hen-Crow did as had been determined; and while the servants of the Prince were searching in the hollow, there they found the Black Snake, which they at once dispatched.

'Said I not well,' continued Damanaka, 'that stratagem excels force?'

'It was well said,' replied Karataka: 'go! and may thy path be prosperous!'

"With that Damanaka repaired to the King, and having done homage, thus addressed him:—

'Your Majesty, there is a dreadful thing on my mind, and I am come to disclose it.'

'Speak!' said the King, with much graciousness.

'Your Majesty,' said the Jackal, 'this Bull has been detected of treason. To my face he has spoken contemptuously of the three prerogatives of the throne ([68]), unto which he aspires.'

"At these words King Tawny-hide stood aghast.

'Your Majesty,' continued Damanaka, 'has placed him above us all in the Court. Sire! he must be displaced!—

> "Teeth grown loose, and wicked-hearted ministers, and poison-trees,
> Pluck them by the roots together; 'tis the thing that giveth ease."

'Good Jackal,' said the King, after some silence; 'this is indeed dreadful; but my regard for the Bull is very great, and it is said,—

> "Long-tried friends are friends to cleave to—never leave thou these i' the lurch:
> What man shuns the fire as sinful for that once it burned a church?"

'That is written of discarding old servants, may it please your Majesty,' observed Damanaka; 'and this Bull is quite a stranger.'

'Wondrous strange!' replied the Lion; 'when I have advanced and protected him that he should plot against me!'

'Your Majesty,' said the Jackal, 'knows what has been written,—

> "Raise an evil soul to honour, and his evil bents remain;
> Bind a cur's tail ne'er so straightly, yet it curleth up again."

"How, in sooth, should Trust and Honour change the evil nature's root?
Though one watered them with nectar (67), poison-trees bear deadly fruit."

I have now at least warned your Majesty: if evil comes the fault is not mine.'

'It will not do to condemn the Bull without inquiry,' mused the King; then he said aloud, 'shall we admonish him, think you, Damanaka?'

'No, no, Sire!' exclaimed the Jackal, eagerly; 'that would spoil all our precautions,—

"Safe within the husk of silence guard the seed of counsel so
That it break not—being broken, then the seedling will not grow."

What is to be done must be done with despatch. After censuring his treason, would your Majesty still trust the traitor?—

"Whoso unto ancient fondness takes again a faithless friend,
Like she-mules that die conceiving, in his folly finds his end."

'But wherein can the Bull injure me?' asked Tawny-hide; 'tell me that!'

'Sire,' replied the Jackal, 'how can I tell it?—

"Ask who his friends are, ere you scorn your foe;
The Wagtail foiled the sea, that did not so."

'How could that be?' demanded King Tawny-hide.

"The Jackal related:—

The Story of the Wagtail and the Sea.

'ON the shore of the Southern Sea there dwelt a pair of Wagtails. The Hen-bird was about to lay, and thus addressed her mate :—

"Husband, we must look about for a fit place to lay my eggs."

"My dear," replied the Cock-bird, "will not this spot do?"

"This spot!" exclaimed the Hen; "why, the tide overflows it."

"Good dame," said the Cock, "am I so pitiful a fellow that the Sea will venture to wash the eggs out of my nest?"

"You are my very good Lord," replied the Hen, with a laugh; "but still there is a great difference between you and the Sea."

'Afterwards, however, at the desire of her mate, she consented to lay her eggs on the sea-beach. Now the Ocean had overheard all this, and, bent upon displaying its strength, it rose and washed away the nest and eggs. Overwhelmed with grief, the Hen-bird flew to her mate, and cried :—

"Husband, the terrible disaster has occurred! My eggs are gone!"

"Be of good heart! my Life," answered he.

'And therewith he called a meeting of fowls, and went with them into the presence of Gurûd, the Lord of the birds (68). When the Master of the Mighty Wing had listened to their complaint, he conveyed it to the knowledge of the God Narayan ([69]), who keeps, and kills, and makes alive the world. The almighty mandate given, Gurûd bound it upon his forehead, and bore it to the Ocean, which, so soon as it heard the will of Narayan, at once gave back the eggs.

'How, indeed,' concluded Damanaka, 'should I judge of the Bull's power, not knowing who supports him?'

'By what signs, then,' asked the King, 'may I conclude him a traitor?'

'If he comes into the presence with his horns lowered for goring, as one that expects the fight. That,' replied the Jackal, 'will convince your Majesty.'

"Thereupon Damanaka the Jackal withdrew, and betook himself towards the Bull, upon perceiving whom he approached slowly, with all the air of one greatly distressed.

'Good master Jackal,' said Lusty-life, 'what goes amiss with thee?'

'All goes amiss with such as serve wicked masters,' replied the Jackal.

'But what ails thee?' asked the Bull.

'Alas!' answered the Jackal, 'what can I say in such a strait!—

> "Even as one who grasps a serpent, drowning in the bitter sea,
> Death to hold and death to loosen—such is life's perplexity."

"And therewithal the Jackal heaved a deep sigh, and squatted down.

'But, good friend,' said the Bull, 'at least tell me what is in thy mind.'

'Bull,' began Damanaka, 'it is a King's secret, and

should not be spoken; but thou didst come here upon my safeguard, and as I hope for the life to come (70), I will tell thee of what touches thee so nearly. Listen!—the heart of the King is turned against thee! he hath sworn secretly that he will kill thee and feast upon thy flesh.'

"Then Lusty-life the Bull was sorely troubled, and he fell a-musing thus,—

"Woman's love rewards the worthless—kings of knaves exalters be;
Wealth attends the selfish niggard, and the cloud rains on the sea."

'Can this be the Jackal's doing?' he reflected. 'Going with honest folk will not make one honest,—

"Many a knave wins fair opinions standing in fair company,
As the sooty soorma pleases, lighted by a brilliant eye."

Then he said aloud, 'wherein can I have angered the King? Do kings hate without cause? I can tell nothing, except that there is no happiness which abides long,—

"Where the azure lotus (71) blossoms, there the alligators hide;
In the sandal-tree are serpents. Pain and pleasure live allied."

I thought his Majesty noble as the sandal-tree; but that, indeed, is not wholly noble,—

"Rich the sandal—yet no part is but a vile thing habits there;
Snake and wasp haunt root and blossom; on the boughs sit ape and bear."

'Bull,' said Damanaka, 'I knew the King of old for one whose tongue was honey and whose heart was poison.'

'But how very hard!' said the Bull, 'that he, being a lion, should attack me, an innocent eater of grass!'

'It is very hard!' said the Jackal.

'Who can have set him against me?' asked the Bull.

'Being so, it cannot be bettered,' replied the Jackal, 'whoever did it,—

> "As a bracelet of crystal, once broke, is not mended;
> So the favour of princes, once altered; is ended."

'Yes,' said the Bull, 'and a king incensed is terrible,—

> "Wrath of kings, and rage of lightning—both be very full of dread;
> But one falls on one man only—one strikes many victims dead."

Still, I can but die—and I will die fighting! When death is certain, and no hope left but in battle, that is the time for war.'

'It is so,' said the Jackal.

"Having weighed all this, Lusty-life inquired of the Jackal by what signs he might conclude the King's hostile intentions.

'If he glowers upon thee,' answered Damanaka, and awaits thee with ears pricked, tail stiffened, paw upraised, and muzzle agape, then thou mayest get thee to thy weapons like a Bull of spirit, for

> "All men scorn the soulless coward who his manhood doth forget:
> On a lifeless heap of ashes fearlessly the foot is set."

"Then Damanaka the Jackal returned to the Lion, and said to him:—

'If it please your Majesty, the traitor is now coming; let your Majesty be on your guard, with ears pricked and paw upraised.'

"The Bull meanwhile approached, and observing the hostile attitude of King Tawny-hide, he also lowered his horns, and prepared for the combat. A terrible battle ensued, and at the last King Tawny-hide slew Lusty-life the Bull. Now when the Bull was dead, the Lion was very sorrowful, and as he sat on his throne lamenting, he said,—

'I repent me of this deed!—

> "As when an Elephant's life-blood is spilt,
> Another hath the spoils (72)—mine is the guilt."

'Sire,' replied the Jackal, 'a King over-merciful is like a Brahman that eats all things equally (73). May all your Majesty's enemies perish as did this Bull.'

"Thus endeth," said the Sage Vishnu-Sárman, "the 'Parting of Friends.'"

"We are gratified exceedingly thereby," replied the Sons of the King.

"Let me then close it thus," said their Preceptor,—

> "So be friendship never parted,
> But among the evil-hearted;
> Time's sure step drag, soon or later,
> To his judgment, such a Traitor;
> Lady Lukshmi, of her grace,
> Grant good fortune to this place;
> And you, Royal boys! and boys of times to be,
> In this fair fable-garden wander free."

War.

WHEN the next day of instruction was come, the King's sons spake to the Sage, Vishnu-Sárman.

"Master," said they, "we are Princes, and the sons of Princes, and we earnestly desire to hear thee discourse upon War."

"I am to speak on what shall please you," replied Vishnu-Sárman. "Hear now, therefore, of 'War,' whose opening is thus:—

"Between the peoples of Peacock and Swan [71]
War raged; and evenly the contest ran,
Until the Swans to trust the Crows began."

"And how was all that?" asked the sons of the Rajah. Vishnu-Sárman proceeded to relate—

The Battle of the Swans and Peacocks.

"IN the Isle of Camphor there is a lake called 'Lotus-water,' and therein a Swan-Royal, named 'Silver-sides,' had his residence. The birds of the marsh and the mere had elected him King, in full council of all the fowls—for a people with no ruler is like a ship that is without a helmsman. One day King Silver-sides, with his courtiers, was quietly reposing on a couch of well-spread lotus-blossoms, when a Crane, named 'Long-bill,' who had just arrived from foreign parts, entered the presence with an obeisance, and sat down.

'What news from abroad, Long-bill?' asked his Majesty.

'Great news, may it please you,' answered the Crane, 'and therefore have I hastened hither. Will your Majesty hear me?'

'Speak!' said King Silver-sides.

'You must know, my Liege,' began the Crane, 'that over all the birds of the Vindhya mountains (75) in Jámbudwipa (76) a Peacock is King, and his name is "Jewel-plume." I was looking for food about a certain burnt jungle there, when some of his retainers discovered me, and asked my name and country. "I am a vassal of King Silver-sides, Lord of the Island of Camphor," I replied, "and I am travelling in foreign lands for my pleasure." Upon that the birds asked me which country, my own or theirs, and which King, appeared to me superior. "How can you ask?" I replied; "the island of Camphor is, as it were, Heaven itself, and its King a heaven-born ruler. To dwellers in a barren land like yours how can I describe them? Come for yourselves, and see the country where I live." Thereupon, your Majesty, the birds were excedingly offended, as one might expect,—

"Simple milk, when serpents drink it, straightway into venom turns;
And a fool who heareth counsel all the wisdom of it spurns."

For, indeed, no reflecting person wastes time in admonishing blockheads—

> "The birds that took the apes to teaching,
> Lost eggs and nests in pay for preaching."

'How did that befall?' asked the King.

The Crane related :—

The Story of the Weaver Birds and the Monkeys.

'IN a nullah that leads down to the Nerbudda river there stood a large silk-cotton tree, where a colony of weaver-birds had built their hanging nests ([77]), and lived snugly in them, whatever the weather. It was in the rainy season, when the heavens are overlaid with clouds like indigo-sheets, and a tremendous storm of water was falling. The birds looked out from their nests, and saw some monkeys, shivering and starved with the cold, standing under the tree. "Twit! twit! you Monkeys," they began to chirrup. "Listen to us!—

> "With beaks we built these nests, of fibres scattered;
> You that have hands and feet, build, or be spattered."

On hearing that the Monkeys were by no means pleased. "Ho! ho!" said they, "the Birds in their snug nests are jeering at us; wait till the rain is over." Accordingly, so soon as the weather mended, the Monkeys climbed into the tree, and broke all the bird's eggs and demolished every nest. I ought to have known better,' concluded the Crane, 'than to have wasted my suggestions on King Jewel-plume's creatures.'

'But what did they say?' asked Silver-sides.

'They said, Rajah,' answered the Crane, "who made that Swan of thine a King?"

'And what was your reply?' asked Silver-sides.

'I demanded,' replied the Crane, 'who made a King of that Peacock of theirs. Thereupon they were ready to kill me for rage; but I displayed my very best valour. Is it not written—

> "A modest manner fits a maid,
> And patience is a man's adorning;
> But brides may kiss, nor do amiss,
> And men may draw, at scathe and scorning."

'Yet a man should measure his own strength first,' said the Rajah, smiling; 'how did you fare against King Jewel-plume's fellows?'

'Very scurvily,' replied Long-bill. "Thou rascal Crane," they cried, "dost thou feed on his soil, and revile our Sovereign? That is past bearing!" And thereat they all pecked at me. Then they began again: "Thou thick-skulled Crane! that King of thine is a goose—a web-footed lord of littleness—and thou art but a frog in a well ([78]) to bid us serve him—him forsooth!—

> "Serving narrow-minded masters dwarfs high natures to their size:
> Seen before a convex mirror, elephants do show as mice."

Bad kings are only strong enough to spoil good vassals—as a fiction once was mightier than a herd of elephants. You know it, don't you?—

"Mighty may prove things insignificant :
A tale of moonshine turned an elephant."

'No! how was that?' I asked.

The birds related—

The Story of the Old Hare and the Elephants.

'ONCE on a time, very little rain had fallen in the due season; and the Elephants being oppressed with thirst, thus accosted their leader:—'Master, how are we to live? The small creatures find something to wash in, but we cannot, and we are half dead in consequence; whither shall we go then, and what shall we do?' Upon that the King of the Elephants led them away a little space; and showed them a beautiful pool of crystal water, where they took their ease. Now it chanced that a company of Hares resided on the banks of the pool, and the going and coming of the elephants trampled many of them to death, till one of their number named Hard-head grumbled out, 'This troop will be coming here to water every day, and every one of our family will be crushed.' 'Do not disquiet yourself,' said an old buck named Good-speed, 'I will contrive to avert it,' and so saying, he set off, bethinking himself on his way how he should approach and accost a herd of elephants; for,

"Elephants destroy by touching, snakes with point of tooth beguile;
Kings by favour kill, and traitors murder with a fatal smile."

'I will get on the top of a hill,' he thought, 'and address the Elephants thence.'

"This being done, and the Lord of the herd perceiving him, it was asked of the Hare, 'Who art thou? and whence comest thou?'

'I am an ambassador from his Godship the Moon,' replied Good-speed.

'State your business,' said the Elephant-king.

'Sire, began the Hare, 'an ambassador speaks the truth safely by charter of his name. Thus saith the Moon, then: "These hares were the guardians of my pool, and thine elephants in coming thither have scared them away. This is not well. Am I not 'Sasanka ([79]), whose banner bears a hare, and are not these hares my votaries?"'

'Please your worship,' said the Elephant-king with much trepidation, 'we knew nothing of this; we will go there no more.'

'It were well,' said the sham ambassador, 'that you first made your apologies to the Divinity, who is quaking with rage in his pool, and then went about your business.'

'We will do so,' replied the Elephant with meekness; and being led by night to the pool, in the ripples of which the image of the Moon was quivering, the herd made their prostrations; the Hare explaining to the Moon that their fault was done in ignorance, and thereupon they got their dismissal."

'Nay,' I said, 'my Sovereign is no fiction, but a great King and a noble, and one that might govern the Three Worlds, much more a kingdom.'

'Thou shalt talk thy treason in the presence,' they

cried; and therewith I was dragged before King Jewel-plume.

'Who is this?' asked the Rajah.

'He is a servant of King Silversides, of the Island of Camphor,' they replied; 'and he slights your Majesty, on your Majesty's own land.'

'Sirrah Crane!' said the Prime Minister, a Vulture, 'who is chief officer in that court?'

'A Brahmany Goose,' I answered, 'named "Know-all;" and he does know every possible science.'

'Sire,' broke in a Parrot, 'this Camphor-isle and the rest are poor places, and belong to Jambu-dwipa. Your Majesty has but to plant the royal foot upon them.'

'Oh! of course,' said the King.

'Nay,' said I, 'if talking makes your Majesty King of Camphor-island, my Liege may be lord of Jambu-dwipa by a better title.'

"And that?' said the Parrot.

'Is fighting!' I responded.

'Good!' said the King, with a smile; 'bid your people prepare for war.'

'Not so,' I replied; 'but send your own ambassador.'

'Who will bear the message?' asked the Rajah. 'He should be loyal, dexterous, and bold.'

'And virtuous,' said the Vulture, 'and therefore a Brahman:—

"Better Virtue marked a herald than that noble blood should deck;
Shiva reigns for ever Shiva while the sea-wave stains his neck (80)."

'Then let the Parrot be appointed,' said the Rajah.

'I am your Majesty's humble servant,' replied the Parrot; 'but this Crane is a bad character, and with the bad I never like to travel. The ten-headed Ravana carried off the wife of Ramchundra (81)! It does not do,

> "With evil people neither stay nor go;
> The Heron died for being with the Crow."

'How did that befall?' asked the King. The Parrot related:—

The Story of the Heron and the Crow.

'THE high-road to Oogein is a very unshaded and sultry one; but there stands upon it one large Peepul-tree (82), and therein a Crow and a Heron had their residence together. It was in the hot weather that a tired traveller passed that way, and, for the sake of the shade, he laid his bow and arrows down, and dropped asleep under the tree. Before long the shadow of the tree shifted, and left his face exposed to the glare; which the Heron perceiving, like the kindly bird he was, perched on the Peepul-tree, and spread his wings out so as to cast a shadow on the traveller's face. There the poor fellow, weary with his travel, continued to sleep soundly, and snored away comfortably with open mouth. The sight of his enjoyment was too much for the malevolent Crow, who, perching over him, dropped an unwelcome morsel into the sleeper's mouth, and straightway flew off. The traveller, starting from his slumber, looked about, and, seeing no bird but the Heron, he fitted an arrow and shot him dead. No!' concluded the Parrot, 'I like the society of honest folk.'

'But why these words, my brother?' I said; his Majesty's herald is to me even as his Majesty.'

'Very fine!' replied the Parrot; 'but—

"Kindly courtesies that issue from a smiling villain's mouth
Serve to startle, like a flower blossoming in time of drouth."

Needs must that thou art a bad man; for by thy talk war will have arisen, which a little conciliation had averted:—

"Conciliation!—weapon of the wise!
Wheedled therewith, by woman's quick device,
The Wheelwright let his ears betray his eyes."

'How came that about?' asked the King. The Parrot related:—

The Story of the Appeased Wheelwright.

'THERE was a Wheelwright in Shri-nuggur, whose name was "Heavy-head." He had good reason to suspect the infidelity of his wife, but he had no absolute proof of it. One day he gave out that he should go to a neighbouring town, and he started accordingly; but he went a very little way, and then returning, hid himself in his wife's chamber. She being quite satisfied that he was really gone away, invited her gallant to pass the evening with her, and began to spend it with him in unrestrained freedom. Presently by chance she detected the presence of her husband, and her manner instantly changed.

"Life of my soul! what ails you?" said her lover; "you are quite dull to-night."

"I am dull," she replied, "because the lord of my life is gone. Without my husband the town is a wilderness. Who knows what may befall him, and whether he will have a nice supper?"

"Trouble thyself no more about the quarrelsome dullard," said her gallant.

"Dullard, quotha!" exclaimed the wife. "What matter what he is, since he is my all? Knowest thou not—

"Of the wife the lord is jewel, though no gems upon her beam;
Lacking him, she lacks adornment, howsoe'er her jewels gleam?"

Thou, and the like of thee, may serve a whim, as we chew a betel-leaf ([83]) and trifle with a flower; but my husband is my master, and can do with me as he will. My life is wrapped up in him—and when he dies, alas! I will certainly die too. Is it not plainly said—

"Hairs three-crore, and half-a-crore hairs, on a man so many grow—
And so many years to Swaga shall the true wife surely go?"

And better still is promised; as herein—

"When the faithful wife ([84]), embracing tenderly her husband dead,
Mounts the blazing pile beside him, as it were the bridal-bed;
Though his sins were twenty thousand, twenty thousand times o'ertold,
She shall bring his soul to splendour, for her love so large and bold."

All this the Wheelwright heard. "What a lucky fellow I am," he thought, "to have a wife so virtuous," and rushing from his place of concealment, he exclaimed in ecstasy to his wife's gallant, "Sir! saw you ever truer wife than mine?"

"When the story was concluded," said Long-bill, "the King, with a gracious gift of food, sent me off before the Parrot; but he is coming after me, and it is now for your Majesty to determine as it shall please you."

"My Liege," observed the Brahmany-goose with a sneer, "the Crane has done the King's business in foreign parts to the best of his power, which is that of a fool."

"Let the past pass," replied the King, "and take thought for the present."

"Be it in secret, then, your Majesty," said the Brahmany-goose—

"Counsel unto six ears spoken, unto all is notified:
When a King holds consultation, let it be with one beside."

Thereupon all withdrew, but the Rajah and the Minister.

"What think you?" said Silver-sides.

"That the Crane has been employed to bring this about," replied the other.

"What shall we do?" asked the King.

"Despatch two spies—the first to inform and send back the other, and make us know the enemy's strength or weakness. They must be such as can travel by land and water, so the Crane will serve for one, and we will keep his family in pledge at the King's gate. The other must be a very reserved character; as it is said—

"Sick men are for skilful leeches—prodigals for prisoning—
Fools for teachers—and the man who keeps a secret, for a King."

"I know such an one," said his Majesty, after a pause.

"It is half the victory," responded the Minister.

At this juncture a chamberlain entered with a profound obeisance, and announced the arrival from Jambudwipa of the Parrot.

"Let him be shown to a reception-room," commanded the Goose, in reply to a look from the King. "He shall presently have audience."

"War is pronounced, then," said the King, as the attendant withdrew.

"It is offered, my Liege; but must not be rashly accepted," replied the other—

> "With gift, craft, promise, cause thy foe to yield;
> When these have failed thee, challenge him a-field."

To gain time for expedients is the first point. Expedients are good for great and little matters equally, like

> "The subtle wash of waves, that smoothly pass,
> But lay the tree as lowly as the grass."

Let his Excellency the Parrot, then, be cajoled and detained here, while we place our fort in condition to be useful. Is it not said—

> "Ten true bowmen on a rampart fifty's onset may sustain;
> Fortalices keep a country more than armies in the plain?"

And your Majesty," continued the Goose, "will recall the points of a good fortress,—

> "Build it strong, and build it spacious, with an entry and retreat;
> Store it well with wood and water, fill its garners full with wheat."

"Whom, then, shall we entrust with this work?" asked King Silver-sides.

"The Paddy-bird ([85]) is a good bird, and a skilful," replied his Minister.

"Let him be summoned!" said the King. And upon the entrance of the Paddy-bird, the superintendence of the fortress was committed to him, and accepted with a low prostration.

"As to the fort, Sire!" remarked the Paddy-bird, "it exists already in yonder large pool; the thing is to store the island in the middle of it with provisions,—

"Gems will no man's life sustain;
Best of gold is golden grain."

"Good!" said King Silver-sides; "let it be looked to." Thereupon, as the Paddy-bird was retiring, the Usher entered again, and making prostration, said: "May it please your Majesty, the King of all the Crows, Night-cloud by name, has just arrived from Singhaladwipa, ([86]) and desires to lay his homage at your Majesty's feet."

"He is a wise bird, and a far-travelled," said the King; "I think we must give him audience."

"Nevertheless, Sire," interrupted the Goose, "we must not forget that he is a land-bird, and therefore not to be received as a water-fowl. Your royal memory doubtless retains the story of

"The Jackal's fate, who being coloured blue,
Leaving his party, left his own life too."

"No! How was that?" asked King Silver-sides.

The Goose related—

The Story of the Dyed Jackal.

"A JACKAL once on a time, as he was prowling about the suburbs of a town, slipped into an indigo-tank; and not being able to get out he laid himself down so as to be taken for dead. The dyer presently coming, and finding what seemed a dead Jackal, carried him into the jungle and then flung him away. Left to himself, the Jackal found his natural colour changed to a splendid blue. 'Really,' he reflected, 'I am now of a most magnificent tint; why should I not make it conduce to my elevation?' With this view, he assembled the other Jackals, and thus harangued them:—

'Good people, the Goddess of the Wood, with her own divine hand, and with every magical herb of the forest, has anointed me King. Behold the complexion of royalty!—and henceforward transact nothing without my imperial permission.'

"The Jackals, overcome by so distinguished a colour, could do nothing but prostrate themselves and promise obedience. His reign, thus begun, extended in time to the lions and tigers; and with these high-born attendants he allowed himself to despise the Jackals, keeping his own kindred at a distance, as though ashamed of them. The Jackals were indignant, but an old beast of their number thus consoled them:—

'Leave the impudent fellow to me. I will contrive his ruin. These tigers and the rest think him a King, because he is coloured blue; we must show them his true colours. Do this, now!—in the evening-time come close about him, and set up a great yell together—he is sure to join in (⁸⁷), as he used to do,—

> "Hard it is to conquer nature: if a dog were made a King,
> Mid the coronation trumpets he would gnaw his sandal-string."

And when he yells the Tigers will know him for a Jackal and fall upon him.'

"The thing befell exactly so, and the Jackal," concluded the Minister, "met the fate of one who leaves his proper party."

"Still," said the King, "the Crow has come a long way, and we might see him, I think."

"Admit the Parrot first, Sire," said the Goose; "the fort has been put in order and the spy despatched."

'Thereupon a Court was called, and the Parrot introduced, followed by Night-cloud the Crow. A seat was offered to the Parrot, who took it, and, with his beak in the air, thus delivered his mission:—

"King Silver-sides!—My master, the King Jewel-plume, Lord of Lords, bids thee, if life and lands be dear to thee, to come and make homage at his august feet; and failing this to get thee gone from Camphor-island."

"Shiva!" exclaimed the Rajah, "is there none that will silence this traitor?"

"Give the sign, your Majesty," said the Crow, starting up, and I will despatch this audacious bird."

"Sir," said the Goose, "be calm! and Sire, deign to listen,—

"'Tis no Council where no Sage is—'tis no Sage that fears not Law;
'Tis no Law which Truth confirms not—'tis no Truth which Fear can awe."

An ambassador must speak unthreatened,—

"Though base be the Herald, nor injure nor let,
For the mouth of a king is he;
The sword may be whet, and the battle set,
But the word of his message goes free."

Thereat the Rajah and Night-cloud resumed their composure; and the Parrot took his departure, escorted by the Minister, and presented with complimentary gifts of gold and jewels. On reaching the palace of Jewel-plume, the King demanded his tidings, and inquired of the country he had visited.

"War must be prepared, may it please you," said the Parrot: "the country is a country of Paradise."

"Prepare for war, then!" said the King.

"We must not enter on it in the face of destiny," interposed the Vulture-Minister, whose title was "Far-sight."

"Let the Astrologer then discover a favourable conjuncture for the expedition, and let my forces be reviewed meantime," said the King.

"We must not march without great circumspection," observed Far-sight.

"Minister!" exclaimed the King, "you chafe me. Say, however, with what force we should set out."

"It should be well selected, rather than unwieldy," replied the Vulture—

"Better few and chosen fighters than of shaven-crowns a host,
For, in headlong flight confounded, with the base the brave are lost."

And its commanders must be judiciously appointed; for it is said—

> "Ever absent, harsh, unjustly portioning the captured prey—
> These, and cold or laggard leaders, make a host to melt away."

"Ah!" interrupted the Rajah, "what need of so much talk? We will go, and, if Váchaspati (88) please, we will conquer."

Shortly afterwards the Spy returned to Camphor-island. "King Silver-sides," he cried, "the Rajah, Jewel-plume, is on his way hither, and has reached the Ghauts (89). Let the fort be manned, for that Vulture is a great minister; and I have learned, too, that there is one among us who is in his pay."

"King!" said the Goose, "that must be the Crow."

"But whence, then, did he show such willingness to punish the Parrot?" objected his Majesty. "Besides, war was declared long after the Crow came to Court."

"I misdoubt him," said the Minister, "because he is a stranger."

"But strangers surely may be well-disposed," replied the King. "How say the books?—

> "Kind is kin, howe'er a stranger—kin unkind is stranger shown;
> Sores hurt, though the body breeds them—drugs relieve, though desert-grown."

Have you never heard of King Sudraka and the unknown Servant, who gave his son's life for the King?"

"Never," answered the Goose.

The Story of the Faithful Rajpoot.

"I WILL tell you the tale," said the King, "as I heard it from 'Lilyflower,' daughter of the Flamingo 'White-flag,' of whom I was once very fond :—A soldier presented himself one morning at King Sudraka's gate, and bade the porter procure an audience for 'Vira-vara, a Rajpoot' (90), who sought employment. Being admitted to the presence, he thus addressed the King :—

'If your Highness needs an attendant, behold one!'

'What pay do you ask?' inquired the King.

'Five hundred pieces of silver a-day,' said Vira-vara.

'And your accoutrements?' asked the King.

'Are these two arms, and this sabre, which serve for a third,' said Vira-vara, rolling up his sleeve.

'I cannot entertain you,' rejoined his Majesty; and thereupon the Rajpoot made salaam, and withdrew. Then said the Ministers, 'If it please your Majesty, the stipend is excessive, but give him pay for four days, and see wherein he may deserve it.' Accordingly, the Rajpoot was recalled, and received wages for four days, with the complimentary betel (91).—Ah! the rare betel! Truly say the wise of it—

"Betel-nut is bitter, hot, sweet, spicy, binding, alkaline—
A demulcent—an astringent—foe to evils intestine;
Giving to the breath a fragrance—to the lips a crimson red;
A detergent, and a kindler of Love's flame that lieth dead.
Praise the gods for the good Betel!—these be thirteen virtues given,
Hard to meet in one thing blended, even in their happy heaven."

"VIRA-VARA REQUESTED TO KNOW HER NAME, AND WHY SHE THUS LAMENTED."

"Now the King narrowly watched the spending of Vira-vara's pay, and discovered that he bestowed half in the service of the Gods and the support of Brahmans, a fourth part in relieving the poor, and reserved a fourth for his sustenance and recreation. This daily division made, he would take his stand with his sabre at the gate of the palace; retiring only upon receiving the royal permission.

"It was on the fourteenth night of the dark half of the month ([92]) that King Sudraka heard below a sound of passionate sobbing. 'Ho! there,' he cried, who waits at the gate?'

'I,' replied Vira-vara, 'may it please you.'

'Go and learn what means this weeping,' said the King.

'I go, your Majesty,' answered the Rajpoot, and therewith departed.

"No sooner was he gone than the King repented him of sending one man alone into a night so dark that a bodkin might pierce a hole in it, and girding on his scimitar, he followed his guard beyond the city gates. When Vira-vara had gone thus far he encountered a beautiful and splendidly-dressed lady who was weeping bitterly; and accosting her, he requested to know her name, and why she thus lamented.

'I am the Fortune ([93]) of the King Sudraka,' answered she; 'a long while I have lived happily in the shadow of his arm; but on the third day he will die, and I must depart, and therefore lament I.'

'Can nothing serve, Divine Lady, to prolong thy stay?' asked the Rajpoot.

'It might be,' replied the Spirit, 'if thou shouldst cut

off the head of thy first-born Shaktidhar, that hath on his body the thirty-two auspicious marks ([34]) of greatness. Were his head offered to the all-helpful Durga, the Rajah should live a hundred years, and I might tarry beside him.'

"So speaking, she disappeared, and Vira-vara retraced his steps to his own house and awoke his wife and son. They arose, and listened with attention until Vira-vara had repeated all the words of the vision. When he had finished, Shaktidhar exclaimed, 'I am thrice happy to be able to save the state of the King. Kill me, my father, and linger not; to give my life in such a cause is good indeed.' 'Yes,' said the Mother, 'it is good, and worthy of our blood; how else should we deserve the King's pay?' Being thus agreed, they repaired together at once to the temple of the Goddess Durga, and having paid their devotions and entreated the favour of the deity on behalf of the King, Vira-vara struck off his son's head, and laid it as an offering upon the shrine. That done, Vira-vara said, 'My service to the King is accomplished, and life without my boy is but a burden,' and therewith he plunged his sword in his own breast and fell dead. Overpowered with grief for her husband and child, the mother also withdrew the twice-blooded weapon, and slew herself with it on the bodies of Vira-vara and Shaktidhar.

"All this was heard and seen by King Sudraka, and he stood aghast at the sad sight. 'Woe is me!' he exclaimed,—

"Kings may come, and Kings may go;
What was I, to bring these low?
Hearts so noble, pierced for me,
Were not, and will never be!"

What reck I of my realm, having lost these?' and thereat he drew his scimitar to take his own life also. At that moment there appeared to him the Goddess, who is Mistress of all men's fortunes. 'Son,' said she, staying his lifted hand, 'forbear thy rash purpose, and bethink thee of thy kingdom.'

"The Rajah fell prostrate before her, and cried,—'O Goddess! I am done with life and wealth and kingdom! If thou hast compassion on me, let my death restore these faithful ones to life; otherwise I follow the path they have marked.' 'Son,' replied the Goddess, 'thine affection is pleasing to me: be it as thou wilt! The Rajpoot and his house shall be rendered alive to thee.' Then the King departed, and presently saw Vira-vara return, and take up again his station as before at the palace-gate.

'Ho! there, Vira-vara!' cried the King, 'what meant the weeping?'

'Let your Majesty rest well!' answered the Rajpoot, 'it was a woman who wept, and was comforted on my approach.' This answer completed the Rajah's astonishment and delight; for we know—

> "He is brave whose tongue is silent of the trophies of his sword;
> He is great whose quiet bearing marks his greatness well assured."

So when the day was come, he called a full council, and, declaring therein all the events of the night, he invested the faithful guard with the sovereignty of the Carnatic.

"Thus, then," concluded King Silver-sides, "in entertaining strangers a man may add to his friends."

"It may well be," replied the Goose; "but a Minister

should advise what is expedient, and not what is pleasing in sentiment:—

"When the Priest, the Leech, the Vizier of a King his flatterers be,
Very soon the King will part with health, and wealth, and piety."

"Let it pass, then," said Silver-sides, "and turn we to the matter in hand. King Jewel-plume is even now pitched under the Ghauts. What think you?"

"That we shall vanquish him," replied the Goose; "for he disregards, as I learn, the counsel of that great statesman, the Vulture Far-sight; and the wise have said,—

"Merciless, or money-loving, deaf to counsel, false of faith,
Thoughtless, spiritless, or careless, changing course with every breath,
Or the man who scorns his rival—if a prince should choose a foe,
Ripe for meeting and defeating, certes he would choose him so."

He is marching without due preparation; let us send the Paddy-bird at the head of a force and attack him on his march."

Accordingly the Paddy-bird, setting out with a force of water-fowl, fell upon the host of the Peacock-king, and did immense execution. Disheartened thereat, King Jewel-plume summoned Far-sight his Minister, and acknowledged to him his precipitation.

"Wherefore do you abandon us, my father?" he said. "Correct for us what has been done amiss."

"My Liege," replied the Vulture, "it has been well observed,—

"By the valorous and unskilful great achievements are not wrought;
Courage, led by careful Prudence, unto highest ends is brought."

You have set Strength in the seat of Counsel, your

Majesty, and he hath clumsily spoiled your plans. How indeed could it fall otherwise? for,—

"Grief kills gladness, winter summer, midnight-gloom the light of
day,
Kindnesses ingratitude, and pleasant friends drive pain away;
Each ends each, but none of other surer conquerers can be
Than Impolicy of Fortune—of Misfortune Policy."

I have said to myself, 'My Prince's understanding is affected—how else would he obscure the moonlight of policy with the night-vapours of talk;' in such a mood I cannot help him,—

"Wisdom answers all who ask her, but a fool she cannot aid;
Blind men in the faithful mirror see not their reflection made."

And therefore I have been absent."

"My father!" said the King, joining his palms in respect, "mine is all the fault! Pardon it, and instruct me how to withdraw my army without further loss."

Then the Vulture's anger melted, and he reflected,—

"Where the Gods are, or thy Gúrú (95)—in the face of Pain and
Age,
Cattle, Brahmans, Kings, and Children—reverently curb thy rage."

And with a benignant smile, he answered the King thus, "Be of good heart, my Liege; thou shalt not only bring the host back safely, but thou shalt first destroy the castle of King Silver-sides."

"How can that be, with my diminished forces?" asked the Rajah.

"It will come to pass!" answered the Vulture. "Break up to-day for the blockade of the fort."

Now, when this was reported by the spies to King Silver-sides, he was greatly alarmed. "Good Goose!"

said he, "what is to be done? Here is the King of the Peacocks at hand, to blockade us,—by his Minister's advice too."

"Sire," replied the Goose, "separate the efficient and the inefficient in your force; and stimulate the loyalty of the first, with a royal bounty of gold and dresses, as each may seem to merit. Now is the the time for it,—

"Oh, my Prince! on eight occasions prodigality is none—
In the solemn sacrificing, at the wedding of a son,
When the glittering treasure given makes the proud invader bleed,
Or its lustre bringeth comfort to the people in their need,
Or when kinsmen are to succour, or a worthy work to end,
Or to do a mistress honour, or to welcome back a friend."

"But is this expenditure needed?" said the King.

"It is needed, my Liege," said the Goose, "and it befits a Monarch; for,—

"Truth, munificence, and valour, are the virtues of a King;
Royalty, devoid of either, sinks to a rejected thing."

"Let it be incurred then!" replied the King.

At this moment Night-cloud, the Crow, made his appearance. "Deign me one regard, Sire," said he, "the insolent enemy is at our gates; let your Majesty give the word, and I will go forth and show my valour and devotion to your Crown."

"It were better to keep our cover," said the Goose. "Wherefore else builded we this fortalice? Is it not said?—

"Hold thy vantage!—alligators on the land make none afraid;
And the lion's but a jackal when he leaves his forest-shade."

But go, your Majesty, and encourage our warriors."

Thereupon they repaired to the Gateway of the Fort, and all day the battle raged there.

It was the morning after, when King Jewel-plume spake thus to his Minister the Vulture—"Good sir, shall thy promise be kept to us?"

"It shall be kept, your Majesty," replied the Vulture; "storm the fort!"

"We will storm it!" said the Peacock-king. The sun was not well risen accordingly when the attack was made, and there arose hot fighting at all the four gates. It was then that the traitorous Crows, headed by their monarch, Night-cloud, put fire to every dwelling in the citadel, and raised a shout of "The Fort is taken! it is taken!" At this terrible sound the soldiers of the Swan-king forsook their posts, and plunged into the pool.

Not thus King Silver-sides:—retiring coolly before the foe, with his General the Paddy-bird, he was cut off and encircled by the troopers of King Jewel-plume, under the command of his Marshal the Cock.

"My General," said the King, "thou shalt not perish for me. Fly! I can go no farther. Fly! I bid thee, and take counsel with the Goose that Crest-jewel, my son, be named King!"

"Good my Lord," replied the Paddy-bird, "speak not thus! Let your Majesty reign victorious while the sun and moon endure. I am governor of your Majesty's fortress, and if the enemy enter it he shall but do so over my body; let me die for thee, my Master!—

"Gentle, generous, and discerning; such a Prince the Gods do give!"

"That shalt thou not!" replied the Rajah,—

"Skilful, honest, and true-hearted; where doth such a Vassal live?"

"Nay! my royal Lord, escape!" cried the Paddy-bird; a king's life is the life of his people,—

"The people are the lotus-leaves, their monarch is the sun—
When he doth sink beneath the waves they vanish every one.
When he doth rise they rise again with bud and blossom rife,
To bask awhile in his warm smile, who is their lord and life."

"Think no more of me." At this instant the Cock rushing forward, inflicted a wound with his sharp spurs on the person of the King; but the Paddy-bird sprang in front of him, and receiving on his body the blows designed for the Rajah, forced him away into the pool. Then turning upon the Cock, he despatched him with a shower of blows from his long bill; and finally succumbed, fighting in the midst of his enemies. Thus the King of the Peacocks captured the fortress; and marched home with all the treasure in it, amid songs of victory.

Then spake the Princes:—"In that army of the Swans there was no soldier like the Paddy-bird, who gave his own life for the King's."

"There be nowhere many such," replied Vishnu-Sarman; "for

"All the cows bring forth are cattle—only now and then is born
An authentic lord of pastures, with his shoulder-scratching horn." (96)

"It is well spoken," said the Princes.

"But for him that dares to die so," added the Sage, "may an eternal heaven be reserved, and may the lustrous Angels of Paradise, the Apsarasas ([97]), conduct him thither! Is it not so declared, indeed?—

> "When the soldier in the battle lays his life down for his king,
> Unto Swarga's perfect glory such a deed his soul shall bring."

"It is so declared," said the Rajah's sons.

"And now, my Princes," concluded Vishnu-Sarman, "you have listened to 'War.'"

"We have listened, and are gratified," replied the sons of the King.

"Let me end then," said their Preceptor, "with this,—

> "If the clouds of battle lower
> When ye come into your power,
> Durga grant the foes that dare you
> Bring no elephants to scare you;
> Nor the thunderous rush of horses,
> Nor the footmen's steel-fringed forces:
> But overblown by Policy's strong breath,
> Hide they in caverns from the avenging death."

Peace.

WHEN the time came for resuming instruction, the King's sons said to Vishnu-Sarman, "Master, we have heard of war, we would now learn somewhat of the treaties which follow war." "It is well asked," replied the Sage; "listen therefore to 'Peace,' which hath this commencement—

> "*When those great Kings their weary war did cease,*
> *The Vulture and the Goose concluded Peace.*"

"How came that?" asked the Princes.

Vishnu-Sarman related:—

The Treaty between the Peacocks and the Swans.

"SO soon as King Jewel-plume had retreated, the first care of King Silver-sides was the discovery of the treason that had cost him the fort.

'Goose,' he said to his Minister, 'who put the fire

to our citadel, think you? Was it an enemy or an inmate?'

'Sire,' replied the Goose, 'Night-cloud and his followers are nowhere to be seen,—it must needs be his work.'

'It must needs be,' sighed the King, after a pause; 'but what ill-fortune!'

'If it please your Majesty, no,' replied the Minister; 'it is written,—

"'Tis the fool who, meeting trouble, straightway destiny reviles;
Knowing not his own misdoing brought his own mischance the whiles."

You have forgotten the saying,—

"Who listens not, when true friends counsel well,
Must fall, as once the foolish Tortoise fell."

'I never heard it,' said the King. 'How was that?' The Goose related—

The Story of the Tortoise and the Geese.

THERE is a pool in South Behar called the "Pool of the Blue Lotus," and two Geese had for a long time lived there. They had a friend in the pool who was a Tortoise, and he was known as 'Shelly-neck.' It chanced one evening that the Tortoise overheard some fishermen talking by the water. "We will stop here to-night," they said, "and in the morning we will catch the fish, the tortoises, and such like." Extremely alarmed at this, the Tortoise repaired to his friends the Geese, and reported the conversation.

"What ever am I to do, Gossips?" he asked.

"The first thing is to be assured of the danger," said the Geese.

"I *am* assured," exclaimed the Tortoise; "the first thing is to avoid it: don't you know?—

"'Time-not-come' [88] and 'Quick-at-Peril,' these two fishes 'scaped the net;
'What-will-be-will-be,' he perished, by the fishermen beset."

"No," said the Geese, "how was it?" Shelly-neck related:—

The Story of Fate and the Three Fishes.

"IT was just such a pool as this, and on the arrival at it of just such men as these fishermen, that three fishes, who had heard their designs, held consultation as to what should be done.

'I shall go to another water,' said "Time-not-come," and away he went.

'Why should we leave unless obliged?" asked "Quick-at-peril." 'When the thing befalls I shall do the best I can,—

> "Who deals with bad dilemmas well, is wise.
> The merchant's wife, with womanly device,
> Kissed—and denied the kiss—under his eyes."

'How was that?' asked the other fish. Quick-at-peril related :—

The Story of the Unabashed Wife.

'THERE was a trader in Vikrama-poora, who had a very beautiful wife, and her name was Jewel-bright. The lady was as unfaithful as she was fair, and had chosen for her last lover one of the household servants. Ah! womankind!—

"Sex, that tires of being true,
Base and new is brave to you
Like the jungle-cows ye range,
Changing food for sake of change."

Now it befell one day that as Jewel-bright was bestowing a kiss on the mouth of the servant, she was surprised by her husband; and seeing him she ran up hastily and said, "My lord, here is an impudent varlet! he eats the camphor which I procured for you; I was actually smelling it on his lips as you entered." The servant catching her meaning, affected offence. "How can a man stay in a house where the mistress is always smelling one's lips for a little camphor?" he said; and thereat he was for going off, and was only constrained by the good man to stay, after much entreaty. 'Therefore,' said Quick-at-peril, 'I mean to abide here, and make the best I can of what befalls, as she did.'

'Yes, yes,' said What-will-be-will-be, 'we all know

"That which will not be will not be, and what is to be will be:
Why not drink this easy physic, antidote of misery?"

"When the morning came, the net was thrown, and both the fishes inclosed. Quick-at-peril, on being drawn up, feigned himself dead; and upon the fisherman's laying him aside, he leaped off again into the water. As to What-will-be-will-be, he was seized and forthwith despatched.——And that," concluded the Tortoise, "is why I wish to devise some plan of escape."

"It might be compassed if you could go elsewhere," said the Geese, "but how can you get across the ground?"

"Can't you take me through the air?" asked the Tortoise.

"Impossible!" said the Geese.

"Not at all!" replied the Tortoise; "you shall hold a stick across in your bills, and I will hang on to it by my mouth—and thus you can readily convey me."

"It is feasible," observed the Geese, "but remember,

> "'Wise men their plans revolve, lest ill befall;
> The Herons gained a friend, and so, lost all."

"How came that about?" asked the Tortoise. The Geese related:—

The Story of the Herons and the Mongoose. (99)

"AMONG the mountains of the north there is one named Eagle-cliff, and near it, upon a fig-tree, a flock of Herons had their residence. At the foot of the tree, in a hollow, there lived a serpent; and he was constantly devouring the nestlings of the Herons. Loud were the complaints of the parent birds, until an old Heron thus advised them:—'You should bring some fishes from the pool, and lay them one by one in a line from the hole of yonder Mongoose to the hollow where the Serpent lives. The Mongoose will find him when it comes after the fish, and if it finds him it will kill him.' The advice seemed good, and was acted upon; but in killing the Snake the Mongoose overheard the cry of the young Herons; and climbing the tree daily, he devoured all that the Snake had left. Therefore," concluded the Geese, "do we bid

"THEREUPON THE GEESE TOOK UP THE STICK—THE TORTOISE HELD FAST—

you look well into your plan: if you should open your mouth, for instance, as we carry you, you will drop and be killed."

"Am I a fool," cried the Tortoise, "to open my mouth? Not I! Come now, convey me!"

'Thereupon the Geese took up the stick; the Tortoise held fast with his mouth, and away they flew. The country people, observing this strange sight, ran after.

"Ho! ho!" cried one, "look at the flying Tortoise!"

"When he falls we'll cook and eat him here," said another.

"No; let us take him home for dinner!" cried a third.

"We can light a fire by the pool, and eat him," said the first.

'The Tortoise heard these unkind remarks in a towering passion. "Eat me—eat ashes!" he exclaimed, opening his mouth—and down he fell directly, and was caught by the countrymen.——Said I not well,' concluded the Goose-Minister, 'that to scorn counsel is to seek destruction?'

'You have well said,' replied King Silver-sides, disconsolately.

'Yes, your Majesty,' interposed the Crane, who was just returned, 'if the Fort had been cleared, Night-cloud could not have fired it, as he did, by the Vulture's instigation.'

'We see it all,' sighed the King, but too late!'—

> "Whoso trusts, for service rendered, or fair words, an enemy,
> Wakes from folly like one falling in his slumber from a tree."

'I witnessed Night-cloud's reception,' continued the

Crane. 'King Jewel-plume showed him great favour, and was for anointing him Rajah of Camphor-island.'

'Hear you that, my Liege?' asked the Goose.

'Go on; I hear!' said Silver-sides.

'To that the Vulture demurred,' continued the Crane:—'"favour to low persons," he said, "was like writing on the sea-sand. To set the base-born in the seat of the great was long ago declared impolitic,—

"Give mean men power, and give thy throat to the knife;
The Mouse, made Tiger, sought his master's life."

"How was that?" asked King Jewel-plume. The Vulture related,—

The Story of the Recluse and the Mouse.

"IN the forest of the Sage Gautama there dwelt a Recluse named Mighty-at-Prayer. Once, as he sat at his frugal meal, a young mouse dropped beside him from the beak of a crow, and he took it up and fed it tenderly with rice grains. Some time after the Saint observed a cat pursuing his dependant to devour it, whereupon he changed the mouse into a stout cat. The cat was a great deal harassed by dogs, upon which the Saint again transformed it into a dog. The dog was always in danger of the tigers, and his protector at last gave him the form of a tiger—considering him all this while, and treating him withal, like nothing but a mouse. The country-folk passing by would say, 'That a tiger! not he; it is a mouse the Saint has transformed.' And the mouse being vexed at this, reflected, 'So long as the Master lives, this shameful story of my origin will survive!' With this thought he was about to take the Saint's life, when he, who knew his purpose, turned the ungrateful beast by a word to his original shape. Besides, your Majesty," continued the Vulture, "it may not be so easy to conquer Camphor-island,—

"Many fine fishes did the old Crane kill,
But the Crab matched him, maugre all his bill."

"How came that to pass?" asked Jewel-plume.

'The Vulture related :—

The Story of the Crane and the Crab.

"THERE was an old Crane at a mère called Lily-water, in Malwa, who stood one day in the shallows with a most dejected look and drooping bill. A Crab observed him and called out, 'Friend Crane! have you given up eating, that you stand there all day?' 'Nay, sir!' replied the old Crane; 'I love my dish of fish, but I have heard the fishermen say that they mean to capture every one that swims in this water; and as that destroys my hope of subsistence, I am resigning myself to death.' All this the fishes overheard. 'In this matter certainly,' they said, his interest is ours; we ought to consult him; for it is written,—

"Fellow be with kindly foemen, rather than with friends unkind;
Friend and foeman are distinguished not by title but by mind.'

Thereupon they repaired to him: 'Good Crane,' they said, 'what course is there for safety?'

'Course of safety there is,' replied the Crane, 'to go elsewhere; and I will carry you one by one to another pool, if you please.'

'Do so,' said the trembling fishes.

"The Crane accordingly took one after another, and having eaten them returned with the report that he had safely deposited each. Last of all, the Crab requested to be taken; and the Crane, coveting his tender flesh, took him up with great apparent respect. On arriving at the spot, which was covered with fish-bones, the Crab perceived the fate reserved for him; and turning round he fastened upon the Crane's throat and tore it so that he perished."

"Well, but," said King Jewel-plume, "we can make Night-cloud viceroy here, to send over to Vindhya all the productions of Camphor-isle!"

'Then the Vulture Far-sight laughed a low laugh and said,—

> "Who, ere he makes a gain has spent it,
> Like the Pot-breaker (100) will repent it."

"What was that?" asked the King. Far-sight related:—

The Story of the Brahman and the Pans.

"THERE was a Brahman in the city of Vána, whose name was Deva Sarman. At the equinoctial feast of the Dussera, he obtained for his duxina-gift a dish of flour, which he took into a potter's shed; and there lay down in the shade among the pots, staff in hand. As he thus reclined he began to meditate, "I can sell this meal for ten cowrie-shells, and with them I can purchase some of these pots and sell them at an advance. With all that money

I shall invest in betel-nuts and body-cloths and make a new profit by their sale; and so go on trafficking till I get a lakh of rupees—what's to prevent me? Then I shall marry four wives—and one at least will be beautiful and young, and she shall be my favourite. Of course the others will be jealous; but if they quarrel, and talk, and trouble me I will belabour them like this—and this"—and therewith he flourished his staff to such a purpose as to smash his meal-dish and break several of the potter's jars. The potter, rushing out, took him by the throat, and turned him off; and so ended his speculations. I smiled, my Liege," concluded the Vulture, "at your precipitancy, thinking of that story."

"Tell me, then, my Father, what should be done," said the King.

"Tell me first, your Majesty, what took the fortress, strength or stratagem?"

"It was a device of yours," said the King.

"It is well," replied the Minister, "and my counsel now is to return before the rainy season, while we can return; and to make peace. We have won renown and taken the enemy's stronghold; let it suffice. I speak as a faithful adviser; and it is written—

> "Whoso, setting duty highest, speaks at need unwelcome things,
> Disregarding fear and favour, such an one may succour kings."

Oh, my Liege! war is uncertain! Nay, it may ruin victor and vanquished,—

> "Sunda the strong, and giant Upasunda (101),
> Contending, like the lightning and the thunder,
> Slew each the other. Learn, the while you wonder."

"Tell me that," said the King of the Peacocks.

'The Vulture related,—

The Duel of the Giants.

"LONG ago, my Liege, there were two Daityas named Sunda and Upasunda, the which with penance and fasting worshipped that God who wears the moon ([102]) for his forehead-jewel; desiring to win his favour, and thereby the lordship of the Three Worlds. At last the God, propitiated by their devotion, spake thus unto them:—

'I grant a boon unto ye,—choose what it shall be.'

"And they, who would have asked dominion, were suddenly minded of Saraswati ([103])—who reigns over the hearts and thoughts of men—to seek a forbidden thing.

'If,' said they, 'we have found favour, let the Divinity give us his own cherished Parvati ([104]), the Queen of Heaven!'

"Terribly incensed was the God, but his word had passed, and the boon must be granted; and Parvati the Divine was delivered up to them. Then those two world-breakers, sick at heart, sin-blinded, and afire with the glorious beauty of the Queen of Life—began to dispute, saying one to another: 'Mine is she! mine is she!' At the last they called for an umpire, and the God himself appeared before them as a venerable Brahman.

'Master,' said they, 'tell us whose she is, for we both won her by our might.'

"Then spake that Brahman:—

"Brahmans for their lore ([105]) have honour; Kshattriyas for their bravery;
Vaisyas for their hard-earned treasure; Sudras for humility."

Ye are Kshattriyas—and it is yours to fight; settle, then, this question by the sword.'

"Thereupon they agreed that he spoke wisely, and drew and battled; and being of equal force, they fell at the same moment by an exchange of blows. Good my Lord," concluded the Minister, "peace is a better thing than war."

"But why not say so before?" asked Jewel-plume.

"I said it at the first," replied the Minister. "I knew King Silver-sides for a just King, upon whom it was ill to wage battle. How say the Scriptures?—

"Seven foemen of all foemen, very hard to vanquish be:
The Truth-teller, the Just-dweller, and the man from passion free,
Subtle, self-sustained, and counting frequent well-won victories,
And the man of many kinsmen—keep the peace with such as these."

The Swan-king has friends and kinsmen, my Liege:—

"And the man with many kinsmen answers with them all attacks;
As the bambu, in the bambus safely sheltered, scorns the axe."

"My counsel then is that peace be concluded with him," said the Vulture.

"All this King Silver-sides and his Minister the Goose heard attentively from the Crane.

'Go again!' said the Goose to Long-bill, 'and bring us news of how the Vulture's advice is received.'

'Minister!' began the King, upon the departure of the Crane, 'tell me as to this peace, who are they with whom it should not be concluded?'

'They be twenty (106), namely——'

'Tarry not to name them,' said the King; 'and what be the qualities of a good ally?'

'Such should be learned in Peace and War,' replied

the Goose, 'in marching and pitching, and seasonably placing an army in the field; for it is said,—

> "He who sets his battle wisely, conquers the unwary foe;
> As the Owl, awaiting night-time, slew the overweening Crow."

Counsel, my Liege, is quintuple,—Commencing, providing, dividing, repelling, and completing.'

'Good!' said the King.

'Power is triple,' continued the Goose, 'being of Kings, of counsels, and of constant effort.'

'It is so!' said the King.

'And expedients, my Liege,' continued the Goose, 'are quadruple, and consist of conciliation, of gifts, of strife-stirring, and of force of arms; for thus it is written,—

> "Whoso hath the gift of giving wisely, equitably, well;
> Whoso, learning all men's secrets, unto none his own will tell:
> Whoso, ever cold and courtly, utters nothing that offends,
> Such an one may rule his fellows unto Earth's extremest ends."

'Then King Jewel-plume would be a good ally,' observed the Swan-king.

'Doubtless!' said the Goose, 'but elated with victory, he will hardly listen to the Vulture's counsel; we must make him do it.'

'How?' asked the King.

'We will cause our dependant the King of Ceylon, Strong-bill the Stork, to raise an insurrection in Jambudwipa.'

'It is well conceived,' said the King. And forthwith a Crane, named Pied-body, was dismissed with a secret message to that Rajah.

"In course of time the first Crane, who had been sent as a spy, came back, and made his report. He related that the Vulture had advised his Sovereign to summon Night-cloud, the Crow, and learn from him regarding King Silver-sides' intentions. Night-cloud attended accordingly.

'Crow!' asked King Jewel-plume, 'what sort of a Monarch is the Rajah Silver-sides?'

'Truthful, may it please you,' replied the Crow; 'and therewithal noble as Yudhisthira ([107]) himself.'

'And his Minister, the Goose?'

'Is a Minister unrivalled, my Liege,' said the Crow-king.

'But how then didst thou so easily deceive them?'

'Ah! your Majesty,' said the Crow, 'there was little credit in that. Is it not said?—

"Cheating them that truly trust you, 'tis a clumsy villainy!
Any knave may slay the child who climbs and slumbers on his knee."

Besides, the Minister detected me immediately. It was the King whose innate goodness forbade him to suspect evil in another:—

"Believe a knave, thyself scorning a lie,
And rue it, like the Brahman, by-and-by."

'What Brahman was that?' asked the King. Night-cloud replied:—

The Story of the Brahman and the Goat.

'A BRAHMAN that lived in the forest of Gautama, your Majesty. He had purveyed a goat to make pooja (108), and was returning home with it on his shoulder when he was descried by three knaves. "If we could but obtain that goat," said they, "it would be a rare trick;" and they ran on, and seated themselves at the foot of three different trees upon the Brahman's road. Presently he came up with the first of them, who addressed him thus:—"Master! why do you carry that dog on your shoulder?" "Dog!" said the Brahman, "it is a goat for sacrifice!" With that he went on a coss (109), and came to the second knave; who called out—"What doest thou with that dog, Master?" The Brahman laid his goat upon the ground, looked it all over, took it up again upon his back, and walked on with his mind in a whirl; for—

> "The good think evil slowly, and they pay
> A price for faith—as witness 'Crop-ear' may."

'Who was Crop-ear?' asked the King of the Peacocks.

The Story of the Camel, the Lion, and his Court.

'A CAMEL, may it please you,' replied Night-cloud, 'who strayed away from a kafila ([110]), and wandered into the forest. A Lion, named "Fierce-fangs," lived in that forest; and his three courtiers, a Tiger, a Jackal, and a Crow, met the Camel, and conducted him to their King. His account of himself was satisfactory, and the Lion took him into his service under the name of Crop-ear. Now it happened that the rainy season was very severe, and the Lion became indisposed, so that there was much difficulty in obtaining food for the Court. The courtiers resolved accordingly to prevail on the Lion to kill the Camel; "for what interest have we," they said, "in this Browser of thistles?"

"What, indeed!" observed the Tiger; "but will the Rajah kill him after his promise of protection, think you?"

"Being famished he will," said the Crow. "Know you not?—

"Hunger hears not, cares not, spares not; no boon of the starving beg;
When the snake is pinched with craving, verily she eats her egg."

Accordingly they repaired to the Lion.

"Hast brought me food, fellow?" growled the Rajah.

"None, may it please you," said the Crow.

"Must we starve, then?" asked his Majesty.

"Not unless you reject the food before you, Sire," rejoined the Crow.

"Before me! how mean you?"

"I mean," replied the Crow (and he whispered it in the Lion's ear), "Crop-ear, the Camel!"

"Now!" said the Lion, and he touched the ground, and afterwards both ears, as he spoke, "I have given him my pledge for his safety, and how should I slay him?"

"Nay, Sire! I said not *slay*," replied the Crow; "it may be that he will *offer* himself for food. To that your Majesty would not object?"

"I am parlous hungry," muttered the Lion.

'Then the Crow went to find the Camel, and, bringing all together before the King under some pretence or other, he thus addressed him:—

"Sire! our pains are come to nothing; we can get no food, and we behold our Lord falling away,

> "Of the Tree of State the root
> Kings are—feed what brings the fruit."

Take me, therefore, your Majesty, and break your fast upon me."

"Good Crow," said the Lion, "I had liever die than do so."

"Will your Majesty deign to make a repast upon *me?*" asked the Jackal.

"On no account!" replied the Lion.

"Condescend, my Lord," said the Tiger, "to appease your hunger with *my* poor flesh."

"Impossible!" responded the Lion.

'Thereupon Crop-ear, not to be behind in what seemed safe, made offer of his own carcase, which was accepted before he had finished; the Tiger instantly tearing his flank open, and all the rest at once devouring him.

'The Brahman,' continued Night-cloud, 'suspected nothing more than did the Camel; and when the third knave had broken his jest upon him for bearing a dog, he threw it down, washed himself clean of the contamination, and went home; while the knaves secured and cooked his goat.'

'But, Night-cloud,' asked the Rajah, 'how couldst thou abide so long among enemies, and conciliate them?'

'It is easy to play the courtier for a purpose,' said Night-cloud,—

"Courtesy may cover malice; on their *heads* the woodmen bring,
Meaning all the while to burn them, logs and faggots—oh, my King!
And the strong and subtle river, rippling at the cedar's foot,
While it seems to lave and kiss it, undermines the hanging root."

Indeed, it has been said,—

"A wise man for an object's sake
His foe upon his back will take,
As with the Frogs once did the Snake."

'How was that?' asked the Peacock-King. The Crow related:—

The Story of the Frogs and the Old Serpent.

IN a deserted garden there once lived a Serpent, "Slow-coil" by name; who had reached an age when he was no longer able to obtain his own food. Lying listlessly by the edge of a pond, he was descried by a certain Frog, and interrogated,—

"Have you given up caring for food, Serpent?"

"Leave me, kindly Sir," replied the subtle reptile; "the griefs of a miserable wretch like me cannot interest your lofty mind."

"Let me at least hear them," said the Frog, somewhat flattered.

"You must know, then, gracious Sir," began the Serpent, "that it is now twenty years since here, in Brahmapoora, I bit the son of Kaundinya, a holy Brahman; of which cruel bite he died. Seeing his boy dead, Kaundinya abandoned himself to despair, and grovelled in his distress upon the ground. Thereat came all his kinsmen, citizens of Bramahpoora, and sat down with him, as the manner is,—

"He who shares his brother's portion, be he beggar, be he lord,
Comes as truly, comes as duly, to the battle as the board;
Stands before the King to succour, follows to the pile to sigh;
He is friend and he is kinsman—less would make the name a lie."

Then spoke a twice-passed Brahman (111), Kapila by name, 'O Kaundinya! thou dost forget thyself to lament thus. Hear what is written—

"Weep not! Life the hired nurse is, holding us a little space;
Death, the mother who doth take us back into our proper place."

"Gone, with all their gauds and glories: gone, like peasants, are the Kings,
Whereunto the world is witness, whereof all her record rings."

What, indeed, my friend, is this mortal frame, that we should set store by it?—

"For the body, daily wasting, is not seen to waste away,
Until wasted, as in water set a jar of unbaked clay."

"And day after day man goeth near and nearer to his fate,
As step after step the victim thither where its slayers wait."

Friends and kinsmen—they must all be surrendered! Is it not said—

"Like as a plank of drift-wood
Tossed on the watery main,
Another plank encountered,
Meets,—touches,—parts again;
So tossed, and drifting ever,
On life's unresting sea,
Men meet, and greet, and sever,
Parting eternally."

Thou knowest these things, let thy wisdom chide thy sorrow, saying—

> "Halt, traveller! rest i' the shade: then up and leave it!
> Stay, Soul! take fill of life; nor losing, grieve it!"

But in sooth a wise man would better avoid love; for—

> "Each beloved object born
> Sets within the heart a thorn,
> Bleeding, when they be uptorn."

And it is well asked—

> "When thine own house, this rotting frame, doth wither,
> Thinking another's lasting—goest thou thither?"

What will be, will be; and who knows not—

> "Meeting makes a parting sure,
> Life's is nothing but death's door."

For truly—

> "As the downward-running rivers never turn and never stay,
> So the days and nights stream deathward, bearing human lives away."

And though it be objected that—

> "Bethinking him of darkness grim, and death's unshunnëd pain,
> A man strong-souled relaxes hold, like leather soaked in rain."

Yet is this none the less assured, that—

> "From the day, the hour, the minute,
> Each life quickens in the womb;
> Thence its march, no falter in it,
> Goes straight forward to the tomb."

Form, good friend, a true idea of mundane matters; and bethink thee that regret is after all but an illusion, an ignorance—

"An 'twere not so, would sorrow cease with years?
Wisdom sees right what want of knowledge fears."

"Kaundinya listened to all this with the air of a dreamer. Then rising up he said, 'Enough! the house is hell to me—I will betake me to the forest.'

'Will that stead you?' asked Kapila; 'nay—

"Seek not the wild, sad heart! thy passions haunt it;
Play hermit in thine house with heart undaunted;
A governed heart, thinking no thought but good,
Makes crowded houses holy solitude."

To be master of one's self—to eat only to prolong life—to yield to love no more than may suffice to perpetuate a family—and never to speak but in the cause of truth, this,' said Kapila, 'is armour against grief. What wouldst thou with a hermit's life—prayer, and purification from sorrow and sin in holy streams? Hear this!—

"Away with those that preach to us the washing off of sin—
Thine own self is the stream for thee to make ablutions in:
In self-restraint it rises pure—flows clear in tide of truth,
By widening banks of wisdom, in waves of peace and ruth.
Bathe there, thou son of Pandu! (112) with reverence and rite,
For never yet was water wet could wash the spirit white."

Resign thyself to loss. Pain exists absolutely. Ease what is it but a minute's alleviation?'

'It is nothing else,' said Kaundinya: 'I will resign myself!' Thereupon," the Serpent continued, "he cursed me (113) with the curse that I should be a carrier of frogs, and so retired—and here remain I to do according to the Brahman's malediction."

'The Frog, hearing all this, went and reported it to Web-foot the Frog-King, who shortly came himself for an excursion on the Serpent. He was carried delightfully, and constantly employed the conveyance. But one day observing the Serpent to be sluggish, he asked the reason.

"May it please you," explained the Serpent, "your slave has nothing to eat."

"Eat a few of my frogs," said the King. "I give you leave."

"I thank your Majesty!" answered the Serpent, and forthwith he began to eat the frogs, until the pond becoming clear, he finished with their monarch himself. 'I also,' said Night-cloud, 'stooped to conquer, but King Silver-sides is a good King, and I would your Majesty were at peace with him.'

'Peace!' cried King Jewel-plume, 'shall I make peace with my vassal! I have vanquished him—let him serve me!'

"At this moment the Parrot came in. 'Sire!' said he, breathlessly, 'the Stork Strong-bill, Rajah of Ceylon, has raised the standard of revolt in Jambu-dwipa, and claims the country.'

'What! what!' cried the King in a fury.

'Excellent good, Goose!' muttered the Minister. 'This is thy work!'

'Bid him but await me!' exclaimed the King, 'and I will tear him up like a tree!'

'Ah, Sire,' said the Minister—

> "Thunder for nothing, like December's cloud,
> Passes unmarked: strike hard, but speak not loud."

We cannot march without making peace first; our rear will be attacked.'

'Must it be so?' asked the King.

'My Liege, it must,' replied the Vulture.

'Make a peace then,' said the King, 'and make an end.'

'It is well,' observed the Minister, and set out for the Court of the King Silver-sides. While he was yet coming, the Crane announced his approach.

'Ah!' said the Swan-King, 'this will be another designing spy from the enemy.'

'Misdoubt him not!' answered the Goose, smiling, 'it is the Vulture Far-sight, a spirit beyond suspicion. Would your Majesty be as the Swan that took the stars reflected in the pool for lily-buds, and being deceived, would eat no lily-shoots by day, thinking them stars?'

'Not so! but treachery breeds mistrust,' replied the Rajah; is it not written—

"Minds deceived by evil natures, from the good their faith withhold;
When hot conjee once has burned them, children blow upon the cold."

'It is so written, my Liege,' said the Minister. 'But this one may be trusted. Let him be received with compliments and a gift.'

"Accordingly the Vulture was conducted, with the most profound respect, from the fort to the King's audience-hall, where a throne was placed for him.

'Minister,' said the Goose, 'consider us and ours at thy disposal.'

'So consider us,' assented the Swan-King.

'I thank you,' said Far-sight; 'but—

"With a gift the miser meet;
Proud men by obeisance greet;
Women's silly fancies soothe;
Give wise men their due—the truth."

'I am come to conclude a peace, not to claim your kingdom. By what mode shall we conclude it?'

'How many modes be there?" asked King Silver-sides.

'Sixteen,' replied the Vulture.

'Are the alliances numbered therein?' asked the King.

No! these be four,' answered the Vulture, 'namely —of mutual help—of friendship—of blood—and of sacrifice.'

'You are a great diplomatist!' said the King. 'Advise us which to choose!'

'There is no Peace like the Golden "Sangata," which is made between good men, based on friendly feeling, and preceded by the Oath of Truth,' replied the Vulture.

'Let us make that Peace!' said the Goose. Far-sight accordingly, with fresh presents of robes and jewels, accompanied the Goose to the camp of the Peacock-King. The Rajah, Jewel-plume, gave the Goose a gracious audience, accepted his terms of Peace, and sent him back to the Swan-King, loaded with gifts and kind speeches. The revolt in Jambu-dwipa was suppressed, and the Peacock-King retired to his own kingdom.

"And now," said Vishnu-Sarman, "I have told your Royal Highnesses all. Is there anything remaining to be told?"

"Reverend Sir!" replied the Princes, "there is nothing. Thanks to you, we have heard and comprehended the perfect cycle of kingly duty, and are content."

"There remains but this, then," said their Preceptor:

"Peace and Plenty, all fair things,
Grace the realm where ye reign Kings;

Grief and loss come not anigh you,
Glory guide and magnify you;
Wisdom keep your statesmen still
Clinging fast, in good or ill,
Clinging, like a bride new-wed,
Unto lips, and breast, and head:
And day by day, that these fair things befall,
The Lady Lukshmi give her grace to all."

NOTES

NOTES.

(1.)

Honour to Gunesh.—Gunesh, or Gunputtee, is the God of Prudence, whom the Hindoos invoke at the outset of all undertakings. His image, having four hands, and the head of an elephant with one tusk, surmounts the portal of a Hindoo residence, as the guardian of the household.

(2.)

A city named Pataliputra.—Now Patna, near the confluence of the Soane and Ganges.

(3.)

The sacred writings.—The Vedas, or holy book of India. They are four in number, and are called the Rig-Veda, Yajur-Veda, Sama-Veda, and Atharva-Veda. Hymns and metrical addresses to the elemental gods occupy them mainly.

(4.)

Childless art thou? . . . .
Less thy misery than his is, who is father to a fool.

The force of this comparison is only perceived by recollecting the extreme anxiety of the Hindoo to obtain, and leave behind him, male offspring. The Sanskrit word *putra* (son) is declared to be a contraction from *puttra*, which means a deliverer from the hell *put*; and the simple performance of the funeral "shraddh" (a libation by a son) is held sufficient to procure repose for the spirit of his departed father. The Hindoo proverb says, "Whoso begetteth a son, planteth a tree, and diggeth a well; that man shall rest in Heaven."

K

(5.)

Sesasum.—The "tilla" seed; which, together with the cocoa-nut, supplies Hindostan with oil.

(6.)

Pundits.—Learned men.

(7.)

The angel of the planet Jupiter.—Vrihaspati, the Instructor of the gods. Like the rest of the Hindoo divinities, he casts no shadow in moving, his eternally watchful eyes never even wink with fatigue, and the crown of flowers on his head blooms in perpetual beauty and freshness.

(8.)

The silk-cotton tree.—Sans. "Shálmali."

(9.)

His radiance the moon.—The moon (Chandra) is a masculine deity in Hindoo mythology. The white lotus opens its blossoms at night only, hence his descriptive epithet.

(10.)

A crow.—The Indian crow is everywhere seen and heard in India. Its plumage is black, with a dull grey hood extending over the head and neck.

(11.)

God of Death.—Yama, called here Kritanta, or the "End-bringer." He is God of Justice as well as of Death, and sits in judgment upon disembodied souls in his infernal city of Yamapoora. Thence he dismisses them upwards to Swarga, downwards to Naraka, or back again to earth in the form of some animal.

(12.)

Bangle.—The bracelet, in one solid piece, of gold, silver, brass, glass, or earthenware, worn by all Indian women.

(13.)

An old tiger.—It is true to nature that an "old tiger" should be the villain of this episode, and devour the traveller; for it is generally when the tiger has lost his teeth and claws by age, and with them his power of securing antelopes, cattle, &c., that he becomes a professed man-stealer. The popular notion was that the hide of a "man-killer" became worn and mangy as a punishment for attacking man, his lord; but it is not until his hide thus assumes the aspect of old age that he has recourse to such easy but illicit food.

(14.)

Kusa grass.—Used in many religious observances by the Hindoos. (*Poa cynosuroides.*)

(15.)

Cows, Brahmans, and men.—The tiger justifies his self-condemnation by confessing to one of the greatest moral guilts possible, the slaughter of cows—a sin all but inexpiable.

(16.)

Son of Kûnti.—Kûnti was wife of Pándu, and mother of the Pandava princes of the *Mahabharata.*

(17.)

Neither give, &c.—Here, and elsewhere, the intelligent reader will remark a curious similarity between these ancient Hindoo proverbs and those of Solomon.

(18.)

Vanish in the dragon's jaw.—Rahoo, an evil spirit, with the tail of a dragon, was held to be the cause of eclipses, by swallowing occasionally the moon and sun. The legend had this origin. At the time when the gods were drinking the nectar, churned from the ocean by the direction of Vishnu, Rahoo insinuated himself among them, and began to drink. The sun and moon, as guardians for the gods, observed the intrusion and revealed it. Vishnu at once cut off the head of the venturous devil, but as the "amrit" drink had rendered him immortal the head and tail retained their separate life, and were placed in the stellar sky. Rahoo, therefore, still mindful of the injury done him by the sun's interference, loses no opportunity of enclosing his ancient enemy in his jaws.

(19.)

Can a golden deer, &c.—An allusion to an episode in the great poem of the Ramayana. Manicha takes the form of a golden deer, in pursuing which Rama is led away insensibly from his abode, and Rávana comes as a beggar and carries off Sita in his absence.

(20.)

The three wide worlds.—Heaven, earth, and the lower regions.

(21.)

The king of the mice.—The mouse, as vehicle of Gunesh, is an important animal in Hindu legend.

(22.)

Sickness, anguish, bonds, and woe,
Spring from wrongs wrought long ago.

By this theory of a series of existences continued until the balance is just, and the soul has purified itself, the Hindoo accounts for the origin of evil. Every fault must have its expiation, and every higher faculty its development; pain and misery being signs of and ordeals in the trial, which is to end in the happy re-absorption of the emancipated spirit.

(23.)

Champak-grove.—The champak is a bushy deciduous tree, bearing a profusion of white star-like blossoms with golden centre, and of the most pleasing perfume.

(24.)

Fig-tree (Sans. "Parkti").—A large handsome tree, with leaves curiously waved.

(25.)

The moon-penance.—A religious observance, inculcated by Manu. The devotee commences the penance at the full moon with an allowance of fifteen mouthfuls for his food, diminishing this by one mouthful each day, till on the fifteenth it is reduced to one. As the new moon then increases, his allowance also ascends to its original proportion.

(26.)

Brahmacharya.—A votary of the Vedas, a name technically applied to young Brahmins after their investiture with the sacred cord, and generally to pundits and Vedic professors.

(27.)

Agni is the twice-born's master.—Agni, the deity of Fire, under his manifestations of light, the sun, &c., occupies a large portion of the Vedic liturgy. The twice-born is the Brahman, whose second birth is dated from his investiture with the "sacred thread."

(28.)

Krishna.—The god Vishnoo under his most celebrated and popular form. He is represented as of a handsome and graceful person, with the dark blue complexion which the name implies.

(29.)

Unto Swarga, &c.—Heaven, the paradise of Indra, and the happy abode of the souls of the just and of the gods.

(30.)

And the castor-oil's a tree, where no tree else its shade affords.

The castor plant, although not altogether a shrub, seldom assumes the proportions and dignity of a tree. It either grows thick as a bush, or shoots up to twelve or sixteen feet, like a sapling.

(31.)

Oil of sandal-wood.—An extract from the well-known fragrant tree of India.

(32.)

The prince of all the serpents.—Vásuki, or Ananta, the chief of the human-headed serpents, who people Pátála, or the regions under the earth.

(33.)

Hari's name and Hara's.—The first is the god Vishnoo, the second Shiva.

(34.)

And to taste the salt of service.—Italian scholars will recall the sorrowful lines of Dante, so nearly resembling these—

"Tu proverai siccome sa di sale
Lo pane altrui, e com 'e duro Caso
Lo scendere e l' salir per l'altrui scale."

DANTE, *Paradiso*, cant. 17.

(35.)

Breathe he like a blacksmith's bellows.—This implement in India is a sewn goat skin, inflated with one hand and noisily emptied by the other.

(36.)

The last thunder.—Alluding to the "Pralaya," or termination of one of the Kalpas of the world's existence.

(37.)

Resolved into the five elements.—The five constituent ingredients of the body. A common periphrasis for death in Sanskrit writings.

(38.)

Lakshmi.—The wife of Vishnoo, Goddess of beauty and abundance. She sprang, like Aphrodite, from the sea, when the gods churned it with the mountain Mandara to obtain the "Amrit," or nectar.

(39.)

New corn.—The Hindoos are as fond, as the English learn to become, of the green ear of the jowaree stalk parched and eaten hot with butter and pepper.

(40.)

A deer named Dapple-back.—Antelopes are common in all parts of India. The true deer, such as the sambur, is found in the forests only.

(41.)

The Koïl.—The black or Indian cuckoo.

(42.)

The god of the five shafts.—"Kama," the Indian Cupid. His bow is made of flowers, the string is a row of bees, and he wounds with five arrows, typifying the five senses. He is known, also, as *Manmatha*, the heart-shaker; *Manasija*, the heart-begotten; and *Ananga*, the bodiless. The second title refers to his reputed origin from the heart of Brahma, though the god is also represented as the son of Lukshmi and Vishnoo. He is called the Bodiless, from a misadventure with Shiva, whom he dared to aim at, but the indignant deity reduced the archer to cinders with one glance of his central eye. He is painted as a handsome boy, riding on a parrot, and surrounded by maidens, who bear his banner with the fish *Makara*.

(43.)

The forest of Brahma.—A wood where the Vedas are read and expounded. A Hindoo Academe.

(44.)

The reverential prostration of the eight members.—The salutations of India are Spanish in their variety and exactness. The "salaam" is universal; but the native greets his neighbour with the more cordial "ram-ram," and receives it with gratification from the Sahib. The better hand must always be employed, and is raised pressed to the palm of the other to perform a "namuskar," the salutation of a Brahman. The prostration alluded to in the text is performed by lowering at once to the ground the hands, breast, forehead, eyes, two knees, and two feet.

(45.)

The moment of fortunate conjunction.—The astrologer is an important personage in every Hindoo town or village to decide upon lucky or unlucky days. The rules for his decision are freely given by Manu. "The day of new moon," he says, "destroys the spiritual teacher (or gooroo), the fourteenth is bad for the learner, and nothing in the Vedas read on the eighth day and the day of full moon will be remembered."

(46.)

A vow to Gauri.—"The fair goddess," *i.e.* Párvati, wife of Shiva.

(47.)

He, whose forehead-jewel is the moon.—Shiva.

(48.)

The soorma.—(Unjun.) The antimony powder used universally by Hindoo women to darken the lids and lashes of the eye. It is applied with a small stick rubbed upon the powder, and a little consequently goes a long way.

(49.)

Chatty.—The large earthen pot employed to hold water.

(50.)

Seeing how the ant-hill grows.—In the great plains of India the large ant-hills form a marked feature. They are thrown up with great rapidity, and have been seen to rise by a public road to the height of three feet or more in a night.

(51.)

The chattra.—The white umbrella borne above the heads of Indian rajahs. and especially appropriated to royalty, like the Chowri or Yak-tail.

(52.)

The retreat of Dhurmma.—Personified virtue, under the form of the bull of Shiva.

(53.)

Káyeth caste.—A writer; a man sprung from a Kshattriya father and a Sudra mother.

(54.)

Washerman.—The labour of the laundry in India is always performed on hard rocks by the river side, and principally by men called "dhobies."

(55.)

Starve thy maw, &c.—(Literally, "with the belly serve the Eater of oblations"—*hutáshan*), *i.e.* stint thyself to perform the sacrifice.

(56.)

Vrihaspati the Grave.—Regent of the planet Jupiter, and Instructor of the divinities.

(57.)

In the north.—There are no lions in India, excepting that called "the maneless lion," occasionally met with in Guzerat.

(58.)

The King of Chedi.—Shishupála; he took also the forms of Ravana and of Hiranya Kasipu, to oppose Krishna, who killed him.

(59.)

Gunpattee.—Gunesh; the deity of prudence. Born from the bathing-water of the Goddess Parvati.

(60.)

A cowry.—The little sea-shell used in India for small change. About 6,000 go to the rupee.

(61.)

The tree of Paradise.—A tree growing in Indra's Swarga, which instantly produced whatever was desired.

(62.)

The form called Gundharva.—Manu, in his Book III., gives the form of eight different kinds of marriage. This is that without ceremonies, and by mutual consent. The ordinary Hindoo rite is very graceful, and resembles in some points the classic custom. At any time after the "Moonj," or investiture with the sacred thread, the Brahman boy is marriageable, and the girl must not be ten years old. They meet at the bride's house, the *laganpatrica* or "marriage horoscope" having been previously made out by the astrologer. There they go through the *suptupadi*, walking together three times round a fire, seven steps at each time; then their garments are tied together, and an offering is placed upon the flames, completing the rite. The bride remains at her father's house until the age of twelve or thirteen, when she is claimed by her husband.

(63.)

Cut thy nose off.—The ordinary expedient of an incensed husband in the East.

(64.)

Yama and the seven guardians.—These eight protecting deities rank next below the Hindoo Trinity. They are:—1. Indra, the air; 2. Agni, the fire; 3. Chandra, the moon; 4. Surya, the sun. 5. Pavana, the wind. 6. Yama, the lord of justice and of the lower worlds. 7. Varuna, God of the waters; and 8. Kuvera, the master of wealth.

(65.)

Shaving the head of the barber's wife.—This indignity reduced her to the appearance and the miserable status of a widow.

(66.)

The three prerogatives of the throne.—Regal authority derives its rights from three sources with the Hindoo authors—viz. Power, Prescription or continuance, and Wisdom.

(67.)

Watered them with nectar.—The Greek word *nectar*, and the Sanskrit *amrit*, are alike in their etymology—"the immortal." Both were the food of the undying gods, and the Hindoo deities thus obtained their ambrosia. The Daityas, like the Titans, had waged war upon the divinities (the Asuras), and these last betook themselves to Vishnoo for protection. He bade them cast certain medicinal herbs into the "sea of milk;" then taking Mount Mandara for a churning-stick, and the king of the serpents for the twisting-string, the god began to churn the ocean for nectar. The Daityas themselves aided on promise of sharing in the strength-restoring extract, and stood at the serpent's head while the Asuras worked at the tail. The great Vishnoo also took part in the work as a tortoise, upon whose back the mountain whirled round backwards and forwards. Out of the seething flood there came up at the last a figure robed in white—Dhanwantari, the physician of the gods—who bore in his hands the first cup-full of the *amrit*. From the same ocean also rose the ever-lovely Lukshmi—the marvellous cow, from which all things that could be desired might be milked—

and the *kalkût*, or poison which stained the neck of Shiva. The nectar thus obtained bestowed new vigour on the wearied gods, and was stored up in the moon, where the lunar rays ripen and perfect it.

(68.)

Gurûd, the lord of the birds.—He is the vehicle and the attendant of Vishnoo, and has a human face with the wings of a bird.

(69.)

The god Narayen.—Varuna, god of the world of waters. This Deity is regent of the west, and a lord of punishment, holding a noosed cord, wherewith to bind transgressors beneath the sea. His *váhana*, a vehicle, is the great fish *mukur*. The present age (*kalpa*) of the world is called Váráha, or the boar's, and was initiated by Narayen. "When that supreme lord," says the Vishnoo Pooran, "woke and beheld the universe void, knowing that the earth lay hid within the waters, he assumed the body of a wild boar, and plunging in them raised up the earth till it floated upon the waves." The name Narayen, suggestive of the Greek Nereus, denotes him "whose *progress* (*ayana*) is upon the face of the *waters* (narah)."

(70.)

The life to come.—Literally, "the other world" (*Paralók*).

(71.)

The azure lotus.—The lotus resembles our water-lily, but is more varied in form and colour. There are white, red, blue, and yellow varieties.

(72.)

Another hath the spoils.—There is a belief, constantly occurring in Hindoo writings, that the elephant's head contains precious stones, resembling pearls. The remorseful monarch alludes to this, and compares his conquest to the slaughter of an elephant, which leaves guilt to the lion, and gives the pearls to some chance hunter.

(73.)

"*A Brahman that eats all things equally.*"—This epithet, "*sarwabhaksha*," and the comparison, are very strong, and suffice to quiet King Tawny-hide's conscience. A Brahman who ate flesh would be like the unclean "*Rákshasas*" or demons.

(74.)

Peacock and Swan.—The peacock is wild in most Indian jungles. The swan (Sanscrit, *hansa*) is a species of flamingo of a white colour, with markings of a golden yellow. The voice and gait of a beautiful woman are likened in the Hindoo poets to those of the "Hansa." It is the vehicle of the god Brahma.

(75.)

The Vindhya mountains.—The chain between Hindustan and the south country or Deccan. The name is said to imply that they appear, from their loftiness, to *stop* the sun in his declining course.

(76.)

Jambu-dwipa.—"The land of the rose-apple"—the central of the seven continents, containing the regions known to Hindoo geographers. It may not be out of place to sketch in this note the Hindoo's cosmogony. He reads in his Poorans that Priyavrata, son of the Self-born, grieving to see the earth but half illumined at one time by the sun, drove round it seven times in his own flaming chariot, the wheels of which formed seven ruts, which are now the beds of the seven oceans. The continents thus divided are also seven. Jambu-dwipa is the central one, with Mount Meru for its own centre, where "men are born of the colour of burnished gold, and the women resemble blue lotuses; where all live as do the gods, and have the vital forces of 10,000 elephants."

Around *Jambu-dwipa* runs a sea of salt-water, and beyond it lies *Plaksha-dwipa.* There the happy inhabitants know nothing of sickness, and live 5,000 years.

Plaksha-kwipa is divided by a sea of sugar-cane juice from *Shál-mali-dwipa.* The castes of this continent are the tawny, the purple, the yellow, and the red, and in it "the vicinity of the gods is very delightful to the soul."

A sea of wine intervenes between this land and *Kusha-dwipa.* There no one dies; but the gods and gandharvas, the heavenly minstrels, share in the pastimes of the fair and innocent persons who dwell in the land.

Kusha-dwipa is separated from *Krauncha-dwipa* by its sea of ghee, or clarified butter. This last is twice as large as the first, and the inhabitants dwell among its mountains with the immortal gods, whom they regard without fear.

Outside *Krauncha-dwipa* rolls the sea of curds and whey, washing also the shores of *Saka-dwipa*, a favoured land, where there is no vice, nor envy, nor injustice. In the black mountains (Syama) of this country the men are black, and they worship the God Vishnoo, as the sun.

Round the dark shores of *Krauncha-dwipa*, "like an armlet of ivory on a Brahmanee's wrist," flows the sea of milk. It divides this continent from the last and farthest of the seven, the *Pushkara-dwipa*. In the perfect joy of this distant sphere, "there is no distinction of highest and lowest, of killer or slain, of truth or falsehood; the people are of one form with the gods, and too high for duty or observances. Food they consume, but it comes spontaneously to them upon desire, and delicately prepared. There is no evil there, but endless good."

And (for the mind yet unsatiated with receding infinity) beyond *Pushkara* is the sea of fresh water, equal to itself in breadth. Passing that is the *Golden Land*, without inhabitants, and yet beyond it lie the *Loka loka* mountains, dark, immovable, and 10,000 yojans (50,000 miles) high and broad. Outside that darkness is the shell of the mundane egg.

"Of which eggs," concludes the Poorana, "there be thousands, and tens of thousands—yea, a hundred millions of millions!"

(77.)

Their hanging nests.—These birds seem to select the bushes over the mouth of a well, or the slender twigs of a tree, as safe places from the snakes.

(78.)

A frog in a well.—Having no more knowledge than the frog has of light.

(79.)

Am I not Sasanka?—From the Sanskrit—*Śaśa*, a hare.

(80.)

Shiva reigns for ever Shiva, while the sea-waves stain his neck.

At the churning of the waters, along with the "amrita" and the beautiful Lukshmi, came up also a deadly venom (Kalkût), fatal to mortals. To avert its evil influence the god Shiva drank it up; but it was potent enough to stain his throat black or dark-blue, whence his title of "Nilkanta," the blue-throated.

(81.)

The wife of Ramchundra, i.e. Rama, who was absent in the chase of a phantom deer of gold.

(82.)

Peepul tree.—Or "Pimpal," the holy fig.

(83.)

A betal leaf.—The "pan-sooparee," a compound of betel-nut, lime, and cloves, wrapped up in a leaf of the pepper-vine, and chewed by all India.

(84.)

The faithful wife.—By such a death as that alluded to, she earns the title of Sati, the "excellent."

(85.)

The paddy-bird.—The common Indian crane; a graceful white bird, to be seen everywhere, and always, in the interior of Hindostan.

(86.)

Singhala-dwipa.—The "Land of the Lion"—Ceylon.

(87.)

He is sure to join in.—The cry of one jackal at night raises a chorus from all those within hearing.

(88.)

Vachaspati.—Policy, "the Lord of Talk." *Hodiè*, "Government."

(89)

Ghauts.—A word applied to ranges of mountain, by which, as by a *staircase*, the country rises into an elevated region. Also to the step-like path leading over or through the mountains, and to the flight of stairs at a river side landing-place.

(90.)

A rajpoot.—Here synonymous with "Kshattriya," a man of the military caste.

(91.)

The complimentary betel.—The "pan-sooparee" (see note 83), neatly folded into a triangular form, and pierced through by a clove, is handed round at the close of all occasions of ceremony. Judged by its popularity (and not by a first experiment upon it), it deserves the encomium which King Silver-sides cannot repress.

(92.)

The dark half of the month.—The Hindoos divide their month into two divisions of fifteen tithees (or days) each. "*Shood*," the bright half, is occupied by the increase of the moon; and "*Vud*," the dark half, marks the moon's waning. The fourteenth night of the dark half would be intensely dark.

(93.)

The fortune.—The "Lukshmi," the attendant genius.

(94.)

The thirty-two auspicious marks.—This superstition, preserved to us in palmistry, is of common occurrence in the Hindoo writings. In Book 19 of the *Vana-parva* (*Mahabharat*) Vahúka chooses his horses by the ten *avartas*, or marks of excellence. "Never," says King Rituparna—

"Never shall we reach Vidarbha, drawn by steeds so slight and small."

Vahuka replies—

"Two on head, and one on forehead, marks of mettle here be all.
Two on chest, on this and that flank two and two, on crupper one,
These the steeds shall reach Vidarbha long before the day be done."

(95.)

Thy Gúrú.—The spiritual instructor of a young Brahman.

(96.)

With his shoulder-scratching horn.—Large branching horns which reach backward and rub upon his shoulders.

(97.)

The Apsarasas.—The houris of Indra's heaven. They also were produced at the churning of the ocean, in raiment and ornaments of celestial splendour. Their office is to receive into Paradise and to solace there with the delights of love the souls of all who have died fighting bravely. In the "Nala" of the Mahabharat (Book 2) Indra the god is made to say—

"They, the just—the lion-hearted,—Lords, who, never yielding place,
Saw the shaft's descending death-blow—saw, and took it on their face!
Theirs this realm of endless joy is, as the Cow of Plenty mine;
Let them come—the Dead in battle—Lo! I wait them—guests divine."

(98.)

Time not come, &c.—These composite titles may serve as instances of conjoined Sanskrit words. One such in the Champú of Trivikrama contains 118 letters.

(99.)

The Mongoose.—An animal of the weasel kind, very common in India, and valued for its active animosity against all serpents.

(100.)

The Pot-breaker.—This episode is the undoubted origin of "Alnaschar" in the *Arabian Nights;* and of a host of stories and proverbs against the inprudence of "counting chickens before they are hatched."

(101.)

Sunda the Strong, and Giant Upasunda.—Two of the Daityas, the Hindoo Titans who fought against the Suras.

(102.)

That God who wears the Moon.—Shiva.

> "On whose brow the Moon shines brave,
> Like the foam on Gunga's wave."

(103.)

Saraswati.—The wife of Brahma, goddess of speech and eloquence—inventress of the Devanagari character and of the Sanskrit. "Thou," says the Sage Vásistha, addressing her in the *Mahabharat* (Śalya Parva), "art nourishment, radiance, fame, perfection, intellect, light. Thou art speech; thou art Swáha; this world is thine, and thou, in four-fold form, art in all its creatures."

(104.)

Parvati.—The wife of Shiva—another name for Durga, the "Mountain Queen." She is the daughter of Himála, King of the Snowy Hills; and her temple, as at Poona, stands generally on a lofty spot.

(105.)

Brahmans for their lore, &c.—Here is a mention of the our castes, with their distinctive occupations.

(106.)

They be twenty.—I suppress in this place nineteen shlokes, or stanzas, of the original, which enumerate rather tediously the vices or failings to be avoided in an ally.

(107.)

Yudhisthira.—The hero of the *Mahabharat*, who crowns the devotion of his life by refusing to enter Heaven unless his wife and friends share in its felicities with him.

(108.)

Pooja.—Sacrifice.

(109.)

Coss.—Two miles.

(110.)

Kafila.—A caravan.

(111.)

A twice-passed Brahman.—The young Brahman, being invested with the sacred thread, and having concluded his studies, becomes of the second order,—a householder—"grihastha."

(112.)

Thou son of Pandu.—Yudhisthira, titular son of the Prince of Delhi, in the *Mahabharata.*

(113.)

He cursed me.—The power of a Brahman's curse is everywhere illustrated in Hindoo writings. "Carry me to Viswamitra," says Vasistha, "lest he curse thee, O chief of rivers!" (*Mahabharata*—Śalya Parva). These sages transformed each other into birds, by the force of mutual imprecation. *Bhagvata—Pooran*—ix. 7, 6. But Vaswamitra was originally a Kshattriya, and became a Brahman by his austerities only. Vasistha, a true Brahman, resisted by a curse the celestial weapons raised against him. Saktri also, his son, met the King Kalmashapada, and, refusing to yield the path, was struck by him. The Brahman instantly cursed the King to become a man-eater, and the first victim of the imposed propensity was the powerful but improvident Saktri himself (*Mahabharata*, Adi Parva). The ocean, originally fresh and pure, became salt by the power of a Brahmanic imprecation.

THE END.